ARCHIVES OF THE
PARANORMAL

CASE FILES FROM THE PARANORMAL
COUPLE'S HAUNTED MUSEUM

By
Cody Ray DesBiens & Satori Hawes

Foreword By
Jason Hawes, John Zaffis, and Larry & Debbie Elward

EERIE QUILL PUBLISHING

Hope, Rhode Island

ISBN: 979-8-218-61287-0

Library of Congress Control Number: 2025902923

First printing edition 2025

Eerie Quill Publishing
Hope, Rhode Island
EMAIL: eeriequillpublishing@gmail.com

To our family and friends, both present and departed...

Your constant support has been our guiding light in the toughest times. Thank you for standing with us, even when it felt like the world was against us. Your love and encouragement continue to inspire us, and this book is a reflection of your unwavering strength and belief in us.
We love you.

To those that told us we couldn't do it. To the people that dedicated their time to planning our failure...

You inspired us to not only keep going, but to push forward stronger and prouder than ever before. Thank you for helping us make this all happen, and for all that is going to continue to happen moving forward.
All the love to you as well.

CONTENTS

PREFACE

CODY RAY DESBIENS

I've been interested in the paranormal for as long as I can remember, but if I had to pinpoint the moment that truly set me on this path, it would be a night when I was about ten years old.

I wasn't feeling well that evening, and couldn't seem to fall asleep. After what felt like hours of tossing and turning, I did what most young kids do when they're sick—I went to my parents' bedroom, hoping one of them could comfort me. I crawled into bed between them and tried to settle in, but no matter how hard I tried, sleep wouldn't come.

Then, I opened my eyes—and froze.

Around the bed, ten men stood in a perfect circle. At first, my mind struggled to make sense of what I was seeing, but then the realization hit me: I could see right through them. They glowed with an eerie white light, their forms transparent yet so distinct. I remember staring at one of them for a moment, and realizing that I could see the shape of the television right through his head.

They moved in a slow procession—gliding out from the wall on the left side of the headboard, circling the bed, and disappearing into the wall on the right side of the headboard. They never wavered, and never acknowledged me. It was just an endless, silent loop.

As if that wasn't terrifying enough, I noticed something even stranger. Most of them were holding masks up to their faces, as if trying to conceal their features. Others had mouths frozen open in unnatural expressions.

I wanted to scream, to wake my parents—but no sound came out. I elbowed my mom and dad, desperate for them to wake up, but they didn't move. It was as if I was the only person in the world who could see what was happening.

My heart pounded as I squeezed my eyes shut, hoping that when I opened them, they'd be gone. But when I finally dared to look again, they were still there, still moving in their ghostly circle.

In a last-ditch effort to shut it all out, I yanked the covers over my head. That's when I heard it—a low murmur. At first, it was just a whisper, but then it grew louder. They were speaking, all of them at once. The words blended together in an eerie hum. I listened, trying to make sense of what they were saying, but nothing sounded familiar.

I don't remember how the night ended. At some point, exhaustion must have taken over because the next thing I knew, it was morning. The room was normal again, and the men were gone.

I never saw them again, but that night changed me forever. From that moment on, I was consumed by an unshakable curiosity about what I had witnessed. I started devouring every book on ghosts and the paranormal that I could find at the local library. The more I read, the more I realized I wasn't alone—countless people had experienced things they couldn't explain. I needed to understand why.

Thankfully, I wasn't the only one in my family with an interest in the unknown. My mom was just as fascinated by the paranormal. One night, she told me about a new ghost show premiering on television, something she thought I'd love. The year was 2004, and the show was called "Ghost Hunters."

That night, I sat with my mom and watched as a team of ordinary people used cameras and audio recorders to investigate haunted locations. But what stunned me the most? The team—The Atlantic Paranormal Society (TAPS)—was based just a few miles away in Warwick, Rhode Island. It was the first time I realized that investigating the paranormal wasn't just something people read about—it was something real people actually did.

I was hooked. Every Wednesday night, my mom and I watched "Ghost Hunters" together—ironically, in the very same room where I'd had my first paranormal experience. It became our tradition, something I looked forward to every week.

Never in my wildest dreams did I think that years later, I would become a member of that very same team. Or that I would go on to fall deeply in love with, and marry Jason Hawes' daughter. Life has a funny way of working out.

While my mom encouraged my fascination with the paranormal, my grandparents were a little less enthusiastic about the topic. Ironically, though, if it weren't for my grandfather, I might never have developed my interest in haunted objects at all...

My grandparents (on my mom's side) lived below us on the first floor of our old house. They were devout Catholics, and while conversations about ghosts never lasted long with them, they were always supportive of my passion for the paranormal. Whenever I went out to explore a new location, they would wish me well, even if they didn't quite understand my fascination.

Every night, it was routine for me to go downstairs and say goodnight to them. Some nights though, I'd go down just a little too late, and walk in on my grandfather in the middle of his evening prayers.

He would always sit on the edge of his bed, facing a large portrait of Christ, deep in prayer. Not wanting to interrupt, I'd quietly wait in the hallway until he was finished before stepping into the room. Once he was done, he would tell me the story of that portrait—a story I had heard countless times, but never grew tired of.

The portrait had been in our family for generations. My great-great grandfather, Antonio, brought it over to America from Italy in the late 1800s. It had been passed down to his son, Angelo, and continued down the line ever since. But what made it truly special was the story tied to it—one that, believe it or not, had a paranormal element of its own.

My grandfather would tell me how his father Angelo, just like him, prayed in front of that portrait every night before bed. But in the final days of his life, he became deeply afraid of passing away. Then, one evening, after finishing his nightly prayer, something extraordinary happened. He claimed that the image of Christ began to move and speak to him. The conversation was deeply personal, but the message was clear: "everything will be okay." Christ reassured him that when his time came, he would have a peaceful transition.

From that moment on, Angelo's fear was gone. He found peace, and when he eventually passed, it was exactly as he had been told—peaceful and without fear.

The portrait was eventually passed down to my grandfather, Samuel. And even though I had heard this story more times than I could count, I always listened as if it were the first time. There was something about it that captivated me—something that planted the earliest seeds of my fascination with objects that seemed to hold power beyond our understanding.

In 2014, my grandfather passed away. In his final days, he too found great comfort in the portrait. And just like his father, he had an experience that brought him peace. He told us that Christ had spoken to him, reassuring him that his mother would be coming to get him. It was a message that eased his transition, just as it had for Angelo.

That portrait is what first sparked my interest in everyday objects that seem to defy normal reality. It was the inspiration that ultimately led to the creation of our museum.

Today, the portrait is proudly displayed with our collection—not just as a family heirloom, but as a symbol of love, faith, and the comforting reminder that, in the end, everything will be okay.

—Cody

Sacred Heart of Jesus portrait, brought to America by Cody's
second great grandfather

I was introduced to the paranormal field through my father, Jason Hawes—famous paranormal investigator, founder of TAPS (The Atlantic Paranormal Society), and star of the show *"Ghost Hunters"* (2004). To put it simply, I was raised in a world where the paranormal was just another part of everyday life. Investigating was practically a family business, and we have always been dedicated to hearing people, helping people, and finding answers both paranormal and natural. Many people ask me what it was like growing up with a famous father, but the truth is that we never focused on the fame. The only thing I knew growing up was that dad was going to work in order to help people. From this I knew, for certain, that I wanted to be like him when I was older.

Growing up, I had the opportunity to learn the process of investigating firsthand. I had multiple experiences growing up, both aiding in my interest of the subject, and leading my parents to believe that I may have been more in tune with the spiritual world. At a young age I would be taking my brothers investigating throughout the house with flashlights, hoping to find ghosts that I could bring to mom and dad. At one point, my family owned a historic hotel property in New Hampshire, and there would be countless nights in which I would see shadows, hear voices, and try my best to capture a real piece of evidence to show off. These experiences, and multiple others, eventually led me to officially join the TAPS team when I came of age.

I always approached the subject of paranormal with a healthy dose of skepticism. I felt that in order to truly believe, I needed to experience paranormal encounters for myself. That mindset shifted when I met Cody Ray DesBiens, a fellow investigator from Massachusetts, and a member of the TAPS Home-Team. When we first met, Cody was quiet, and seemed to be constantly observing places and people with a curious mind. He always seemed to be focused on finding the logical explanation, but he was open to the possibility that there was no natural explanation. He was kind, and welcoming of my involvement on the team. We clicked instantly, and now looking back, I think there was a reason for it.

The first night we met, there was an investigation event in Bozrah Connecticut, located at an antique store. The TAPS Home-Team was inviting people into the shop, and showing the basics of paranormal investigating. Everyone was so excited to have a chance at exploring the unknown.

I tried to contain it, but admittedly, I was probably the most excited to investigate being outside of my families training wheels. The evening was exceptionally active, but one moment stood out from all others. At one point, Cody and I were talking amongst ourselves, and he said something that had made me burst out laughing. As we laughed, I remember happening to touch his arm and shoulder as we stood next to each other, preparing for the next portion of investigating. When my arm met his, however, a loud series of knocking and banging noises filled the room. It was loud enough to make everyone stop, and the entire paranormal team question what had just taken place. We all thought that the location had just presented major paranormal evidence, and that the shop was a hotspot of intelligent activity. Little did we know, however, that there was more at play. Cody and I, together, would be able to create a connection to the other side. One that has honestly raised more questions than answers as time goes on.

Through my experiences with Cody over the years, my perspective has evolved from needing constant proof to understanding that the spiritual world is real, and that *we must document it whenever possible*. Since meeting Cody, I've delved deep into the realm of spirituality, while also promoting the importance of data and evidence collection. I had started embracing a new approach to the paranormal that I never thought of trying before.

For me, investigating isn't just about communicating with spirits —it's also about listening to people who are experiencing things that they can't explain. People want to know that there are others out there that are willing to believe them, and listen to their valuable insights. I love hearing people's stories, understanding their fears, and doing everything I can to bring peace of mind to them and their families. At the heart of it all, this field isn't just about the unknown—it's about connection, both with the past, and the people living in the present.

—Satori

FOREWORD

BY JASON HAWES, JOHN ZAFFIS,
and REVEREND LARRY & DEBBIE ELWARD

JASON HAWES

The bond between people and objects has always been deeply rooted in history, emotion, and energy. For Satori and Cody, this connection transcends the physical, delving into the mysteries of the paranormal and the stories that linger in the shadows of our everyday lives. Their collection of haunted objects is not just a display of the supernatural—it is a repository of human emotion, history, and the echoes of lives once lived.

This book is a gateway into the extraordinary world that Satori and Cody have carefully cultivated through their passion for the paranormal. Each object they've encountered carries with it not only a tale but a lesson—about life, death, and the enduring presence of the human spirit. The stories behind these artifacts are sometimes chilling, sometimes sad, sometimes amusing, but always deeply fascinating. Through their research and connection to the unseen, Satori and Cody bring these stories to life.

But this book is more than a collection of haunted tales. It's a testament to Satori and Cody's growth as investigators, storytellers, and keepers of the past. Their journey into the paranormal field has been marked by curiosity, compassion, and a desire to bridge the gap between the living and the dead. As they've grown together they've deepened their understanding of the unseen forces that shape our world.

Satori and Cody approach their work with a level of respect and care that sets them apart. Their haunted objects are not just relics, they are connections to those who have passed on, and their stories deserve to be told.

Whether you're an investigator, a curious skeptic, or someone interested in the paranormal, Satori and Cody invite you to explore their world where every object tells a story.

Satori Hawes, Cody Ray DesBiens, and Jason Hawes

Jason Hawes is a paranormal investigator, author, and television personality best known for his lead on the television program "Ghost Hunters." He is also the founder of TAPS (The Atlantic Paranormal Society), and most importantly, Satori's father.

JOHN ZAFFIS, with REVEREND LARRY & DEBBIE ELWARD

One afternoon Debbie and Larry were sitting in John Zaffis' office discussing the events they had witnessed a few days earlier, during their time spent with Cody and Satori. "We really witnessed something special the other day with those two, didn't we?" John asked. Deb and Larry both nodded in agreement. Debbie told them "I was pleasantly surprised that my mother came through, especially the way it happened. After Satori spelled "Patricia," she then spelled out "Chamberlin"...with the 'in'. My mother would always get annoyed with people spelling it wrong... you know with the 'ain' and not with the 'in'. After the reading I felt really, really good. I guess this is how people who attend gatherings with John Edward or James von Prague must feel after a communication is made with a loved one who has passed."

Larry cut in saying "I've been involved with the paranormal for almost as long as John, and I've never seen anything like it. I had heard these *footstep* sounds coming out of nowhere. After this experience, and hearing them with my own ears, I still can't get over it. I could hear the sound clearly, but couldn't pinpoint from where it was coming from. It was like *surround sound* coming from everywhere."

John said "I've known those two since they were kids, and didn't even know they were into the paranormal. And some of the things they came out with were really amazing!" "Like what?" asked Debbie. "I've never seen you so taken aback by someone's reading before." "Well" John said, "the things they brought through were only things family members would know, something that could not have been researched beforehand. Like my uncle Frank saying that he came for my mother when she passed. I was thinking about it while on the computer, and some info came up reminding me it was the anniversary of her passing. What a day for him to come through. That, and all the things my other uncle Ed Warren told us (from the reading)... I mean it was really mind blowing." "Me too," said Debbie. "I'm so pleased that my parents came through. We enjoyed the evening, and can't wait to see them again."

Larry concluded "Those two were the real deal. We've been doing this paranormal stuff for years, and can distinguish the fake and the fraud." Debbie and John agreed, and the three discussed future plans to visit with, and perhaps even collaborate on a project with Cody and Satori.

Reverend Larry & Debbie Elward, Satori Hawes, John Zaffis, and Cody Ray DesBiens

John Zaffis, renowned for his work in the paranormal field, is the star of the television series "Haunted Collector," and the nephew to legendary investigators Ed & Lorraine Warren.
Reverend Larry Elward is a priest and experienced exorcist, while his wife, Debbie Elward, is a gifted clairvoyant and dedicated researcher. Together, they are all accomplished authors, contributing valuable insights to the study of the supernatural.

INTRODUCTION

What does it mean to be haunted? Most people think of dark, abandoned places, old creaky houses, and restless spirits drifting through the night. For us—a couple forever bound by our shared fascination with the supernatural—the paranormal isn't confined to ghost stories and shadowy hallways. It's woven into the fabric of the world around us, hidden in plain sight. It's in the objects that surround us—the forgotten toys, dusty paintings, and everyday items that once held meaning to someone. Some of these objects carry faint echoes of the past, whispering memories of love, loss, or tragedy. Others hold far more sinister attachments—pieces of history that refuse to be left behind, bound by energies that defy explanation.

In early 2019, we embarked on a journey that would redefine our understanding of what it means to be haunted. Both of us have spent years traveling the country—immersed in paranormal investigation, helping scared families, and bearing witness to eerie occurrences that most people would consider the stuff of nightmares. We soon began to realize that spirits aren't limited to the boundaries of old houses or locations. Spirits can sometimes attach themselves to objects, creating energetically charged artifacts that carry with them not only their own histories, but the lingering presence of those who once owned, used, or cherished them.

This interest led us down an extraordinary path, one that would bring us face-to-face with some of the most chilling and enigmatic objects ever encountered. What began as the inheritance of a single, seemingly harmless item—a family heirloom passed down through Cody's side of the family— soon grew into something far larger. Word spread, and before long, people from around the world began reaching out to us, desperate to rid themselves of items they could no longer bear to keep. Dolls that whisper unsettling phrases, paintings that seem to watch you from their frames, mirrors that hold secrets too dark to fathom, and so much more. Soon, a handful of items became a museum full of claimed haunted and cursed pieces. Each item came with a story, and each story was more intriguing than the last.

Over time, this growing museum gained a name. It became The Paranormal Couple's Haunted Museum, a dubbed "foster home" of objects steeped in both mystery and the supernatural. This book is your invitation to take a small step inside our museum to experience its strange and haunted history for yourself. This book is more than just a collection of claims and stories—it's a journey into the origins, unexplainable phenomena, and lingering energies attached to these objects. Through careful research, and extensive investigations, we now offer you a glimpse into our case files. We offer you a view into the mysterious and often terrifying accounts attached to these everyday pieces.

From cursed statues to eerie relics, every item has a tale to tell. Consequently, each tale may just challenge what you think you know about the paranormal.

A word of caution: this book is more than just a simple catalog of supposedly haunted artifacts. These objects carry more than just stories, they carry an essence that is sometimes felt by those who read about them. As you immerse yourself into these accounts, you may find the boundary between the spiritual world and yours beginning to blur. Depending on how sensitive you may be, you may experience strange sensations, fleeting shadows, or an unexplained chill—these are just some of the experiences shared by those who have come into contact with our museum collection. Whether these occurrences are coincidences, or something more, we leave for you to decide.

Each chapter invites you to confront the possibility that ordinary objects can hold extraordinary power, that the things we discard or forget about might hold onto us long after we've let them go. As you turn the pages, you may begin to see the items around you in a different light—your favorite chair, your grandmother's clock, even the trinkets on your desk. Could they hold energies of their own, waiting to reveal their secrets?

Welcome to The Paranormal Couple's Haunted Museum, a place where the past is never truly gone, and where even the smallest trinket can hold unimaginable power. Open this book, if you dare, and take a journey into the haunted world of The Paranormal Couple. This invitation comes with a warning, however, to tread carefully—for once you step into our world, you may find that the objects on display are closer to you than you ever could have imagined...

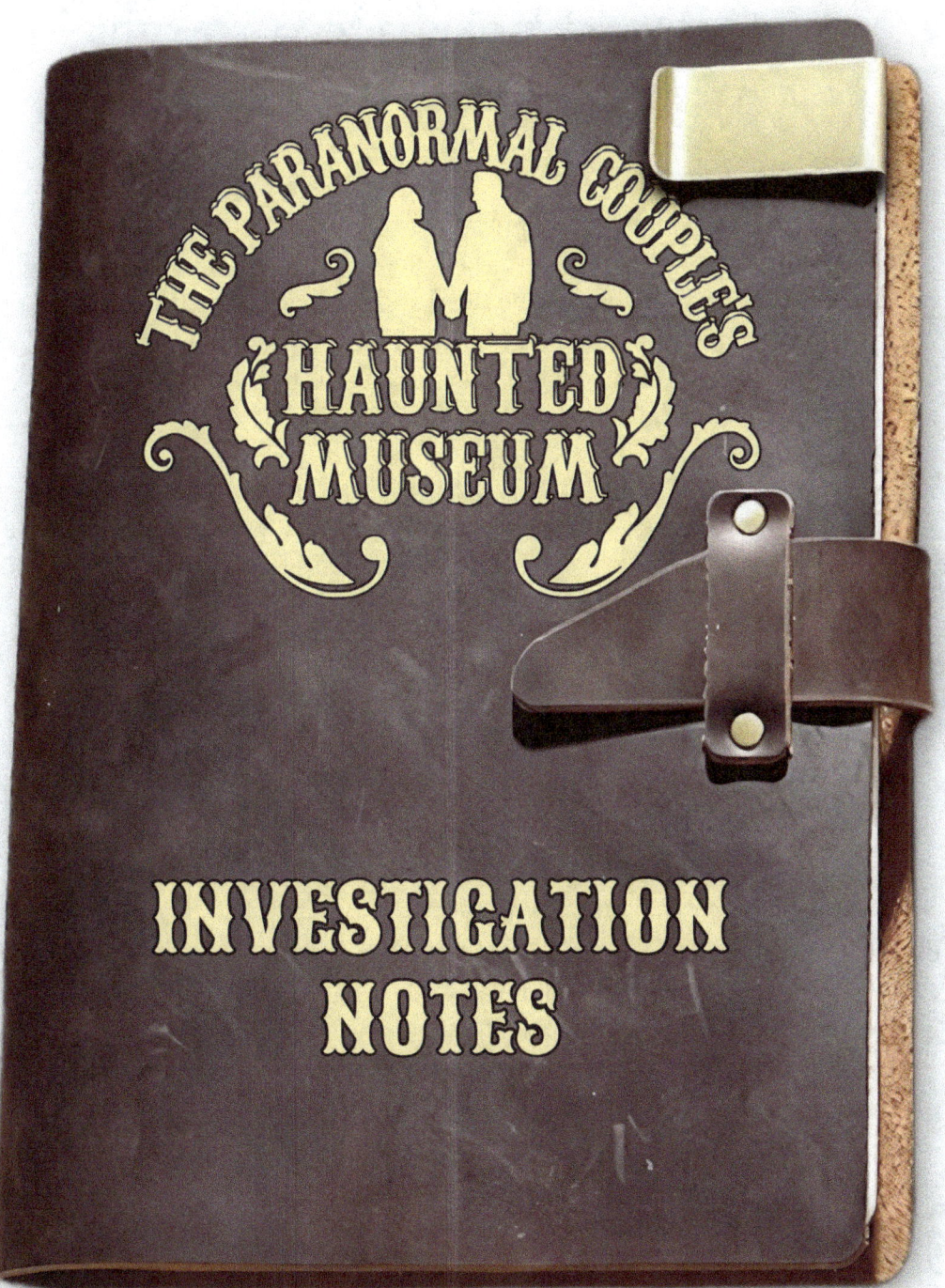

HOW DOES AN OBJECT BECOME HAUNTED?

The way an object feels in your hand can sometimes differ from the predisposed expectations placed upon it. Some things can feel heavier than they should, not because of their material, but due to the invisible energetic weight it may carry. A porcelain doll on a forgotten shelf, its glass eyes clouded with the years, seems to watch when no one is looking. A cracked mirror at a thrift shop reflects shapes that don't quite match reality. A ring, gleaming despite its age, tingles against the skin as though it remembers the touch of another soul.

People often assume that the haunting is tied to the object's age. A relic passed down through centuries that must have accumulated layers of history along the way. These layers being so thick, that it bleeds into the present. But even the newest things—a child's toy fresh from the factory, or a watch bought yesterday, can hum with an uncanny energy, as though these items had become more than they were meant to be.

Many people seem to sense it, instinctively. We call it coincidence, or imagination, but deep down many of us know better. These objects sit in silence, absorbing the world around them, soaking in the laughter and tears, the joy and the anguish of the lives they are exposed to. They are witnesses to moments we both wish we could forget, and others that we wish we would never lose memory of.

But what is it that leaves an object with this strange, unsettling presence? Why do some things seemingly become vessels for something unseen, while others remain ordinary? These questions linger, unanswered yet ever-present. The reasons are not random, nor are they simple. Each object has its story, and its story has its cause.

Some causes lie buried in shadow, their truths obscured by time and distance. Others are sharp, immediate, and undeniable, cutting through the veil of the mundane. But always, there are reasons. And to understand them is to step into a world that many fear to tread.

Here are some of the main ways haunted objects come to be.

Emotional Imprints and Residual Energies

When people experience strong emotions such as love, anger, fear, or grief, those emotions are sometimes believed to leave an "imprint" on the environment or objects exposed nearby. Items that were cherished, hated, or used in pivotal moments (like family heirlooms or personal belongings) are theorized to have an ability to absorb and retain these energies, causing people who encounter them to sense lingering feelings. This type of haunting does not usually include an intelligent spirit, rather, a moment playing itself over like a record when encountered. This is known famously as a "residual haunting." While this type of haunting may not involve an active spirit, people often describe feeling unsettled, sad, anxious, or some form of power around these objects.

Tragic Deaths or Trauma

When a person dies in a traumatic or violent way, their spirit may choose to not fully move on, and it's thought that their presence can become attached to objects that they were close to in life. This can happen with objects found in places of tragedy (like homes or locations with dark histories) or belongings that held sentimental value to the deceased. Such objects might carry the energy of the person or event, causing eerie phenomena such as whispering sounds, cold spots, object movement or manipulation, and more.

Intentional Rituals and Curses

Some objects are haunted or cursed intentionally. Throughout history, people have used ritualistic practices, spells, hexes or curses to bind spirits or energy to specific items as a form of protection, punishment, power or revenge. Items like voodoo dolls, cursed jewelry, and ritual artifacts often fall into this category, deliberately infused with personal intentions or linked to spiritual forces. These items often produce more diverse hauntings, as they were crafted to bring a specific result, either good or negative, to those who possess or come into contact with them.

Possessions and Attachments

Some believe that spirits, or even non-human entities (such as demonic entities, angelic entities, and shadow beings) can attach themselves to objects as a way to stay anchored to the physical world. This is sometimes referred to as a "vessel" haunting. Dolls, mirrors, and jewelry are common vessels because they are frequently handled, creating a physical connection. Dolls are especially associated with the category of object possession and attachment due to their human-like appearance, resembling a human body within this physical world. Hollywood does have a part to play in the portrayal of possessed dolls, however, creating a terrifying and often-times over exaggerated representation of haunted objects. Once attached, these entities are theorized to manifest through the object, causing strange and unsettling events to unfold around it as if the object was alive.

Mourning Practices and Spirit Communication

In the Victorian era and other historical periods, it was common to keep objects associated with deceased loved ones such as locks of hair, personal trinkets, death masks, and more as part of mourning rituals. These keepsakes were meant to preserve the memory of the dead, and even help maintain a spiritual connection to that individual. Sometimes, séances, spirit boards, and other forms of communication with the dead are thought to inadvertently draw in spirits that may not leave when the session ends. This, in turn, transforms the item itself into a haunted object.

Places with High Paranormal Activity

Some objects are merely caught up in the wrong place at the wrong time. On the other hand, others may say that these types of objects are in the right place at the perfect time. Items left in places with high paranormal energy such as battlefields, mass death sites, or notoriously haunted locations, are theorized to have an ability to absorb that energy, and take it with them when removed. People who take "souvenirs" from such locations (especially without permission, which is wrong) often find themselves experiencing such strange occurrences, as if a part of the place followed them home.

Unintentional Hauntings

Occasionally, people inadvertently create haunted objects. A child's doll, for example, may absorb a child's fears, sadness, or loneliness, becoming a comfort object that retains that emotional energy and purpose. In rare cases, a child's imagination or belief in the doll's "aliveness" may act almost like a self-fulfilling ritual, creating a haunting that takes on a life of its own. Similarly, items given as gifts with particularly strong intentions, like passionate love or hatred, can sometimes carry a piece of that emotion long after they're passed on.

THE QUARANTINE ROOM

Every object that arrives at the museum with a claim of paranormal activity must first pass through The Quarantine Room. Tucked away from the main exhibition space, this area is where we observe each item in isolation, attempting to capture its unique paranormal signature. Some people might think it's strange that we'd dedicate an entire room to this, but those who work within the paranormal, especially with problematic items, understand its importance.

Haunted objects are rarely predictable. Some items may arrive with a quiet presence that only reveals itself after weeks, months, or even years from its initial introduction into the museum. Others make their spiritual presence known almost instantly, sometimes before we've even had the opportunity to unbox them. And then there are those that do... nothing at all. That's where The Quarantine Room comes into play. Here, we give each item a controlled and solitary space where it can be observed, measured, and tested to verify the claims of its previous owners.

Once an item is accepted by the museum, it is placed directly into its own quarantine. The small designated room is outfitted with the latest equipment used to detect and document paranormal phenomena. Surveillance cameras cover every angle, capturing video in different light spectrums. Audio recorders with ultra-sensitive microphones are placed in every corner, along with temperature and motion sensors. Even the atmospheric conditions are tracked, in case there is a sudden shift in temperature, humidity, or barometric pressure.

Each object is logged into our system with its reported history as we have been told by the previous owners. We carefully record every detail the client provides about the object: when it was last active, any sounds it has made, movements it has had, even the emotions it seemed to provoke. This is our baseline, a checklist we go through to determine if any of these effects will appear within the two-week quarantine period. Sometimes, items can appear at our doorstep without warning. These items lack information surrounding its history, claims of paranormal activity, or why it was even donated. These cases are trickier, as we have to observe them for longer periods of time with no guiding information.

Most objects, interestingly enough, remain quiet during this time. In the first few days, it's not unusual for nothing to happen at all. It's as though the item needs to "acclimate" to its new surroundings, adjusting to the stillness of the space and controlled conditions of the room. We've learned that paranormal energy doesn't necessarily travel well; sometimes, a haunting clings to a place, not an object.

But not always. Every so often, an object will surprise us, defying patterns and revealing an energy of its own, regardless of its location.

The Quarantine Room has become our reliable gatekeeper. Objects that exhibit major paranormal activity in their former homes might show some trace of it here, if we give them enough time. But there's a second purpose to the room, one we rarely mention to our visitors: We want to make sure we have enough knowledge of the potential haunting, ultimately making sure that these objects don't negatively influence one another.

Once objects leave The Quarantine Room, they are then carefully placed into the main exhibition area. A lot of thought and consideration goes into this process for many reasons. We don't know what could happen if one highly active object were to influence another, or what energies might combine and ignite if two particular items were to closely interact. The quarantine process helps us identify the strongest presences and personalities, and allows us to manage the display accordingly.

Each week, we check our recordings from The Quarantine Room. Most often, it's extremely quiet and uneventful, but some nights, the silence breaks. We may hear the sound of whispers, faint scratching, or a flash of movement across one of our cameras. Those are the nights we feel both a rush of excitement and a familiar chill, the kind that reminds us why this collection started in the first place.

We invite you to turn the page and begin exploring a carefully curated selection of case files, delving just a little deeper into the extraordinary encounters that have crossed our paths. Each tale is a testament to the power of the unknown. We truly hope you enjoy unraveling these mysteries as much as we did investigating them.

THE EDI+ METER

The EDI+ Meter is a comprehensive tool designed and developed by CenTex Paranormal for paranormal investigations. This meter offers multiple environmental sensors and data logging capabilities.

The device's features include:

EMF Detection:
Detects low-frequency EMF down to 10 Hz, providing accurate milligauss readings from 0 to 12 mg.

Environmental Sensors:
Monitors changes in ambient temperature, humidity, and barometric pressure.

Data Logging:
Records all sensor data onto an SD card, allowing for a detailed analysis in the included graphing software.

This tool is essential for monitoring our quarantine room because it allows us to gather detailed environmental data without needing to be present in the room. This helps us minimize exposure to the quarantined environment.

THE PARANORMAL COUPLE'S

"HAUNTED"
MUSEUM
OF

OBJECTS, ODDITIES AND CURIOSITIES

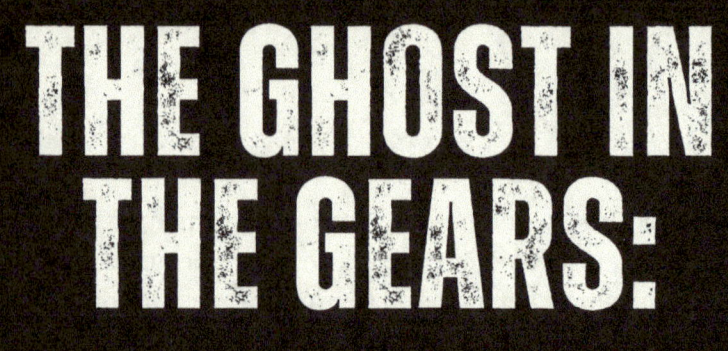

THE GHOST IN THE GEARS:

TIMEPIECES HAUNTED BY THE PAST

CLOCKS

* Some believe that spirits can manipulate clocks to send messages, such as stopping them, changing the time, or causing them to chime unexpectedly.

* Unexplained behavior in a clock is sometimes interpreted as a sign of a deceased loved one attempting to make contact.

* Seeing the same time repeatedly on a clock is often viewed as a spiritual message or synchronicity.

FUN FACT:
Whenever we see 11:11 on a clock, we always make a wish.

Clocks serve as a reminder that time moves forward, indifferent to those who ask it to slow down or halt. Each tick, each turn of the gears, calls attention to the minutes slipping away, and our lives moving forward, moment by moment. In our museum's collection, however, some clocks seem to tell more than just the time. These are clocks with a haunting past—timepieces that tick not just with the hour, but with an echo of memories, as if time itself were somehow caught within the device.

But why clocks? What makes them such compelling vessels for the paranormal? Some believe that clocks are particularly susceptible to spiritual or supernatural energy because they mark a boundary between past, present, and future. Their very nature as keepers of time grants them a profound connection to the concept of mortality, serving as a reminder of life's impermanence. In Chinese folklore, gifting a clock is akin to giving a countdown to death, and stopped clocks are often viewed as omens of ill fortune. In Victorian England, stopping a household clock at the time of death was a common practice, ensuring the soul would not become trapped within the relentless ticking of time. These traditions reflect the universal human fear and fascination with time's inescapable grip.

The symbolism of clocks even bridges into the world of art, serving as a memento mori. This Latin phrase means "remember you must die." Throughout multiple cultures and mediums, clocks are consistently associated with the idea of fleeting time, and life's inevitable end. For those whose lives were cut short, however, the ticking of a clock may feel like an unfinished rhythm, a song abruptly ended.

These haunted timepieces stand as eerie testaments to the idea that time can hold impressions—and sometimes, even spirits. When someone's life is cut short, especially in a sudden or tragic way, they may cling to time itself, unable to let go of the moments that defined their final hours. In such cases, the clock becomes a witness or vessel for a lingering presence, bound by its ticking hands.

Another theory suggests that clocks act as conduits for specific moments imprinted in time. Timepieces may often witness significant events—final words spoken at a bedside, the moments before a tragedy, the celebrations of a life's milestones. The emotional energy of these instances may imprint upon the clock, much like a residual haunting in other objects as previously mentioned. A clock or watch that stops at a pivotal moment, for instance, may be seen as absorbing the intensity of that memory, replaying it in an endless loop. This may also include other activity surrounding the clock such as voices, sensations, visual anomalies, and more. In this sense, the haunted clock is less a symbol of fear and more a guardian of memory, holding on to fragments of time that refuse to fade.

Interestingly, clocks also symbolize control—a notion that becomes haunting in its own right. We rely on clocks to dictate the rhythms of our days, to keep us organized and tethered to the present. But when someone deeply attached to a particular clock or watch passes away, they may continue to assert their influence. By haunting the clock, they resist the natural flow of time, ensuring that their presence and story remain tangible. When the clock stops or behaves erratically, it becomes an assertion that their time is not yet finished, and that their memory endures even in defiance of the ticking hands.

Some haunted clocks seem to have lives of their own. Visitors to our museum exhibitions have reported seeing our haunted clocks' hands move backward, and sometimes stop completely, only to resume normal function later. Others have heard unexplained chiming or ticking in quiet sections, as if the clock itself were alive. These eerie behaviors leave us wondering if the spirits bound to these timepieces are trying to communicate, or if time itself is somehow unraveling in their presence.

Even the design of certain clocks contribute to their haunting aura. Towering grandfather clocks, with their deep chimes and ornate craftsmanship, can feel almost alive. Their imposing forms seem to command attention, demanding recognition of the weight they carry—whether it's time, memory, or something more supernatural. Pocket watches, on the other hand, seem to carry an aura of intimacy. They are often associated with personal stories of love, loss, or tragedy. Each crack in the glass, each worn engraving, tells a story that might still echo within the item itself.

Many visitors to our museum exhibits are surprised to find that our collection of haunted clocks don't simply tell time—they keep something far more profound. For some, they preserve memories, capturing moments of love, loss, and longing. For others, they remind us of the limits of our control over time, and the mysteries that lie just beyond each tick of the hand. These artifacts, along with their ghostly echoes, stand as a bridge between the measurable and the immeasurable, between the living and the dead, holding a space where time and spirit meet.

As you gaze at these haunted clocks, it's worth considering: do they just tell time, or do they tell a story? Do they measure hours, or do they measure the weight of what lingers unseen—the memories, emotions, and entities that refuse to be forgotten? Perhaps in their ticking, there is a lesson for us all: time is not just something to be counted, but something to be respected, cherished, and, in some cases, even feared.

THE WORLD'S MOST HAUNTED CLOCK

Located in Prague, Czech Republic, The Prague Astronomical Clock is steeped in legend and superstition, earning its reputation as one of the most well known haunted timepieces in history. Erected in 1410, it is said to be cursed after its master clockmaker, Hanus, was blinded to prevent him from recreating his handiwork elsewhere. In revenge, Hanus allegedly sabotaged the clock, bringing it to a halt and cursing it. Local lore claims that misfortune falls upon the city whenever the clock stops, as it is said to hold a mystical connection to Prague's fate. Mysterious apparitions and eerie noises near the clock only add to its haunting legacy, drawing curious onlookers and ghost hunters alike.

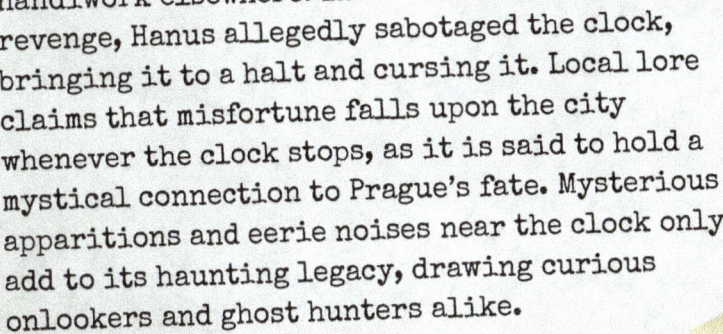

THE STOPPING
CLOCKS

Some objects carry more than just history; they carry a haunting presence that defies explanation. In July 2019, Donna Moore, a longtime resident of Brattleboro, Vermont, reached out to us with a plea for help. Her life had been thrown into turmoil after bringing home two vintage clocks purchased from second-hand stores in her area. What should have been a pair of charming additions to her home, quickly became the source of increasingly bizarre and unsettling events.

Donna described her home as "peaceful" before acquiring the clocks. For nearly two decades, she had lived in her quaint New England home without any notable disturbances. It was a sanctuary, filled with carefully chosen antiques and mementos that reflected her appreciation for history. That sense of tranquility began to unravel when she brought home the second clock, an octagon-shaped wall clock with a yellow wood finish. From the moment it arrived, Donna sensed something was "off," though she couldn't immediately pinpoint what it was.

The shift in energy within her home was subtle at first. It began with unseasonal cold spots in her living room, which was an odd occurrence during the height of summer. Donna tried to brush it off as poor insulation or airflow, but as the weeks went on, the phenomena became harder to explain. Electronic devices in her home started behaving erratically, flickering on and off without warning. Even more unsettling was the distinct smell of cigar smoke that often lingered in the air, a jarring anomaly in a household where no one smoked any substances.

The most chilling aspect of the case involved the clocks themselves. Both the octagon clock and an earlier acquired green tabletop clock inexplicably stopped working at the exact same time, 3:33 a.m., on two separate occasions. Initially, Donna dismissed it as a coincidence. She replaced the batteries and reset both clocks, hoping that would put an end to the strangeness. When it happened a second time, however, her unease grew into outright fear. The repetition of 3:33 seemed too deliberate to ignore.

Donna's apprehension deepened with each passing day. She began experiencing other phenomena that were harder to rationalize. Faint giggles that seemed to echo in the dead of night, shadowy figures darting just out of view, and an unsettling heaviness whenever she entered the room where the clocks were displayed. Adding to her distress, she found herself plagued by persistent headaches whenever she would spend prolonged time near the clocks, as if their presence carried a tangible, oppressive weight.

By the time Donna reached out to us, she was convinced that the clocks were the source of the disturbances. Her email conveyed a growing desperation, describing how she felt watched, vulnerable, and completely out of her depth. She expressed a deep concern regarding the repeated occurrence of the number 333, wondering if it carried a sinister warning or if it was a marker of something greater. The atmosphere of her once peaceful home had become so charged with tension that she had begun spending nights in her guest room just to distance herself from the unsettling energy.

When we arrived at Donna's home, she was visibly relieved to see us. She greeted us at the door with an obvious sense of urgency, and wasted no time in showing us the two clocks which she had already packed into a box and set aside for removal. Although her nerves were evident, Donna graciously allowed us to walk through her home, recounting each event in painstaking detail. She seemed genuinely hopeful that we could help her reclaim the peace she had lost.

Before we had left, I (Cody) performed a brief prayer at Donna's request, asking for protection and peace to fill her home once more. She stood with us, clutching her hands tightly as I spoke the words, and for the first time since we arrived, her shoulders seemed to relax. Her gratitude was evident as we carried the clocks out of her home, though there was still a lingering fear in her eyes, as if part of her expected the disturbances to return.

Upon arriving back at the museum, the clocks were placed in The Quarantine Room, where they began a period of observation. It seemed to be apparent early on that their unsettling influence was far from over. Even within the controlled environment of the museum, there were moments that hinted at the clocks' residual energy. Unexplained cold drafts, minor electrical malfunctions, and the unnerving sense of being watched. It seemed that on certain occasions, there was some sort of energy or entity that had the ability to manipulate both equipment, and human senses.

This case raises complex questions about the residual energy that objects can carry. Are these clocks haunted by a restless spirit, or are they acting as conduits for something more mysterious? Was the appearance of the number 333 a message waiting to be deciphered, or was it merely a coincidence? Donna's experience serves as a chilling reminder that even the most ordinary objects can hide remarkable secrets.

The following pages delve deeper into the evidence, the phenomena, and the details behind Case #071619, The Stopping Clocks.

RESONATING OBJECTS

It is our observation that when multiple haunted objects are placed together, they can sometimes intensify each other's paranormal activity. Here are some possible reasons why:

Energy Amplification:

Spirits or residual energies within different objects may resonate with each other, increasing their overall strength and activity.

Spiritual Networking:

If there are multiple spirits attached to different objects, they may communicate, creating a new phenomenon not previously experienced.

Chain Reaction:

Similar to how certain materials conduct electricity, some objects may act as conduits, allowing energy to transfer between them.

THE PARANORMAL COUPLE'S

HAUNTED MUSEUM

OF

OBJECTS, ODDITIES AND CURIOSITIES

CASE FILE

NAME: THE STOPPING CLOCKS

CASE#: 071619

DATE: July 16, 2019

CASE #: 071619 - The Stopping Clocks

CLIENT NAME: Donna Moore
ALL OCCUPANTS AT LOCATION: Donna (client) lives alone
DATE OF CASE: July of 2019
DATE CLIENT OBTAINED OBJECT: Around July 6, 2019
CLIENT LOCATION: Brattleboro, Vermont
LOCATION OBTAINED: Second hand store
OBJECT MANUFACTURE ORIGIN: None found

POINT OF CONTACT
EMAIL SENT TO PARANORMAL COUPLE ACCOUNT:
From: ********@email.com
Date: July 16, 2019 at 9:53:02 PM EST
To: contact@paranormalcouple.com
Subject: Please Help

Dear Cody & Satori. My name is Donna and I live in Brattleboro Vermont. I am contacting you both because of some unsettling things I have been experiencing here in my home. I live alone and it is very unnerving. I hope you both are able to help me out a bit. Thank you for taking the time to read my message.
My email is ********@email.com.

- Donna

From: contact@paranormalcouple.com
Date: July 16, 2019 at 11:22:01 PM EST
To: *********@email.com
Subject: RE: Please Help

Greetings Donna,

Thank you so much for reaching out to us. We are sorry to hear you are experiencing some unnerving activity. Of course we are willing to help in any way we can. Would you mind speaking on the phone with us to explain what exactly has been happening at your home?

Thank you and talk soon!

Our Best,

Cody & Satori

PRELIMINARY PHONE INTERVIEW

PHONE INTERVIEW BY: Cody Ray DesBiens & Satori Hawes
DATE: July 18, 2019
CLIENT NAME: Donna Moore
PHONE NUMBER: ***-***-****
EMAIL: *********@email.com

DESCRIPTION OF OBJECT IN QUESTION:

- Two vintage clocks.
- One clock is a wall hanging octagon shape that is a yellow / wood color.
- The second clock is a green upright table / mantle clock.

HOW WAS THE OBJECT OBTAINED:

- Both clocks were obtained at two different second hand stores in Vermont on two separate occasions.

WHY DO YOU THINK THE OBJECT IS THE CAUSE OF THE PARANORMAL ACTIVITY:

- The first clock that was purchased and brought home was the green tabletop clock.
- Nothing abnormal or paranormal happened until Donna purchased the second clock shaped like an octagon.
- As soon as the second clock was brought home, the client states that "the feeling in the house had changed. It felt like something was off, but I just couldn't figure out exactly what was wrong."

HOW LONG HAVE YOU BEEN AT THIS LOCATION?:

- Donna states that she has lived at the same location for almost twenty years.
- She explained that she is a big believer in the afterlife, but she had never experienced anything paranormal until she brought the second clock home.

UNEXPLAINED TEMPERATURE CHANGES:

- Donna explained that on a few occasions, the temperature in the home dropped below the set temperature on the thermostat.
- She states that on the second time it occurred, she called the maintenance worker to check on the systems. He found nothing wrong with it.
- Thinking back on it all, at the time she didn't connect the temperature drops with the clock, but now she believes that they are connected with both events that occured with the items.

UNEXPLAINED ANOMALIES WITH ELECTRICAL DEVICES:

- The client states that recently, on multiple occasions, she found her TV turned on when she woke up in the morning.
- Donna states that her TV has never done this before, until the second clock was brought home.
- She also states that her cell phone battery has been draining at an abnormal speed only when she is at home.
- Donna states that sometimes she has to keep her phone plugged in at all times while she is home, so the battery doesn't die completely.

UNEXPLAINED ILLNESS:

- The client states that she has had an abnormal amount of headaches. It seems to only happen when she spends a good amount of time in the room with the octagon clock. This is also the same room with the TV that has been turning on by itself.

MANIPULATION OF OBJECTS:

- On two occasions, Donna has found both clocks stopped at exactly 3:33.
- The second occurrence is what prompted her to contact the museum.
- The first time it happened, she thought it was a fluke, so she changed the batteries out. A few days later, it happened again.
- It is seemingly impossible for two separate clocks to stop at the same time.
- Donna expressed that both occurrences did actually happen at 3:33 in the morning. She noticed that they had stopped after she woke up and checked the time.

UNEXPLAINED ODORS:

- Donna states that she has never smoked a day in her life. Over the past couple of weeks, however, she has been getting a whiff of cigar smoke randomly.
- She states that her windows are always closed because she has the air conditioner on.
- She also states that smoking of any kind is not permitted on her building's property, except for in the designated area which is far from her home.
- Donna expressed that she always tries to cover up the mysterious cigar scent with air fresheners so she doesn't get in trouble with her landlord.

UNEXPLAINED SOUNDS:

- The client reports the sounds of "shuffling noises" on multiple occasions in the middle of the night.
- She states that when she sits up in bed to check on the noise, it immediately stops.
- Donna says that "it seems like whatever it is, is playing games with me."

UNEXPLAINED VOICES:

- The client states that on the first night that the clocks stopped, she heard what seemed like giggling. She states that it sounded like a female.
- She immediately assumed that it was just a loud neighbor, or some other normal explanation.
- The night before the second occurence of the clocks stopping, she heard the laughing sound again while lying down in bed.
- She says that it sounded exactly like the first laughing incident, and as soon as she noticed it, the laughing stopped.
- After this second event, she states that her "gut" told her that it was something, or someone, attached to the clocks.

APPARITIONS/VISUAL ANOMALIES:

- Donna states that on one occasion, she saw "a black shadow mist move across the living room doorway."
- She also states that when she finally processed what she had seen, it had frightened her.

PHYSICAL CONTACT:

- None Reported

OTHER NOTES:

- Donna is worried that whatever is in her home, is something that is malicious.
- She is also concerned that the entity is trying to warn her about something that is related to the number three.

DESIRED RESULT / OUTCOME:

- The client wants the clocks removed from her home as soon as possible.
- Satori and I have instructed her to leave the clocks set at 3:33, remove the batteries, and place the clocks in a box. We also instructed her to place the box within a closet, away from her living space, until we arrived to pick the clocks up.

INVESTIGATOR NOTES:

- I (Cody) have made arrangements to remove the clocks on Saturday, July 20, 2019 at Donna's home in Brattleboro, Vermont.

IN-PERSON VISIT TO LOCATION
DATE OF VISIT: Saturday - July 20, 2019
INVESTIGATORS PRESENT: Cody Ray DesBiens, (Satori Hawes via phone when possible)
LOCATION RESIDENTS PRESENT: Donna (Client)

PRELIMINARY NOTES UPON ARRIVAL:

- The property itself is very nice, and Donna's home is located on the 4th floor of the building.
- Upon driving onto the property, I noticed that the smoking area is located far away from the building. It is located on the far end of the property, a great distance away from Donna's area of the building.
- Donna was very kind and welcoming. She met me (Cody) outside the main door of the building.
- She instructed me (Cody) where to find the box containing the clocks.

CLOSING NOTES OF IN-PERSON VISIT:

- The clocks are now in our possession. I (Cody) ended our visit with Donna by saying a prayer with her. This is because she had requested to ask for protection, and only good spirits to protect her.

<u>**NOTES:**</u>

DATE OF ENTRY TO MUSEUM: Saturday - July 20, 2019
- Today, we placed the clocks within the quarantine room to observe them for the next week or two.
- We have placed the batteries back in the clocks, and set them both to 12:00 to see if they stop at 3:33.

IMPORTANT UPDATE: Sunday - August 4, 2019
- The clocks have been moved out of the quarantine room and placed into "general population."
- We have also removed the batteries to prevent corrosion.

CLIENT FOLLOW UP: Friday - August 9, 2019 - PHONE CALL
- Satori & I were able to reach our client over the telephone.
- Donna stated that her home feels "so much better now" that the clocks are "out of her life."
- She states that she has not had any headaches, smelled any cigar smoke, heard any laughing, or had any issues with her TV.
- She is very thankful for our assistance.
- We have instructed her to contact us if anything changes.

IMPORTANT UPDATE: Saturday - September 28, 2019
- Today, Satori and I were in the museum organizing some items, when we started to hear a random ticking sound.
- We immediately started walking around the museum to find the source, and as we approached the clocks, we noticed that the hand on the octagon clock was ticking by itself.
- As I (Cody) picked the clock up to examine it, the ticking immediately stopped at the exact moment we realized that the clock had no batteries in it.
- We have no explanation as to why this happened.

IMPORTANT UPDATE: Sunday - September 18, 2022

- This weekend, we had the clocks, along with a few other items, on display at a local event.
- Two separate individuals, at two separate times, approached us stating that they had seen the second hand move on one of the clocks.
- When I (Cody) examined the clocks a second time, I noticed that the second hand on the octagon clock had moved slightly since the last time I had checked it.

IMPORTANT UPDATE: Saturday - November 4, 2023

- Today, the clocks were on display at a paranormal conference in New Jersey.
- Throughout the day, we had hundreds of individuals walk through our exhibit room to read about the items we had brought from the museum collection.
- On two separate occasions, two unrelated individuals once again claimed to see the hands of the clock move. They claimed that this movement occurred while they were reading the display story located directly in front of the clocks, situated on the exhibit table.
- We are unable to definitively confirm any movement of the clock hands at this time.

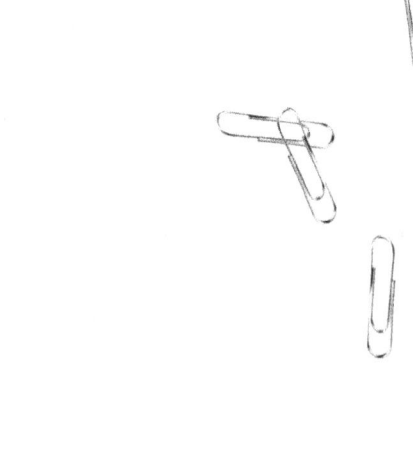

Seeing the number "333" is often interpreted as a spiritual, or symbolic message. This is depending on your beliefs and context. Here are some common interpretations:

Alignment and Support
In spiritual traditions, "333" is often associated with divine protection and guidance. It suggests that the universe, angels, or spiritual guides are supporting you. It can be a sign to trust that you are on the right path and that help is available if needed.

Balance and Harmony
The number 3 often represents balance and wholeness in connection to mind, body, and spirit or past, present, and future. Seeing "333" may be a reminder to seek balance in your life, and focus on areas that feel out of sync.

Spiritual Awakening
For some, "333" is also a sign of spiritual growth or awakening. It can indicate that you're being called to deepen your connection to your higher self, or the spiritual realm.

Consider keeping a journal of when and where you see repeating numbers to uncover patterns or messages.

333

THE PECULIAR PENDULUM

It had been an ordinary summer evening when Sharon Brown found the clock. She was driving home along a quiet suburban road with the windows down, and the warm breeze flowing through her hair. The rhythmic hum of insects, and the smooth movements of the car provided a relaxing commute. All of this changed, however, when her attention caught something unusual.

Nestled between a trash bin, and a cardboard box stood the clock. It was unlike anything she had seen before. It was an intricately carved wooden device, its polished surface glinting in the fading sunlight. Sharon felt an inexplicable pull, as if the clock were calling to her. She pulled over, stepped out of her car, and allowed her curiosity to overpower any possible hesitation.

Up close, the clock was even more mesmerizing. Its overlay exhibited a delicate carving of a face, almost too pristine for something discarded as trash. She admired the craftsmanship. Sharon didn't know much about antiques, but she knew that this was special, too beautiful, and too well preserved to be left for the garbage truck.

Without giving it a second thought, she carried the clock to her car and continued to drive the rest of the way home. She was eager to find it a proper place in her house. She cleaned it carefully, removing a light layer of dust, and set it upon her living room mantel right above the fireplace. Its intriguing presence immediately transformed the space, adding a sense of charm and character. For the first few hours, everything seemed perfectly normal. But as the sun dipped below the horizon, the atmosphere in her home began to change.

It started with a chill, a sudden biting cold that crept into the living room. Sharon initially dismissed it as a draft, even as her thermostat displayed a steady 70 degrees. Her dog, however, reacted differently. Normally a friendly, curious companion, the dog soon began avoiding the living room entirely. He wouldn't cross the threshold, even when coaxed with treats. Instead, he would sit outside of the room, staring intently at the mantel.

Over the next few days, the peculiarities grew harder to ignore. The once lovely living room felt heavy and oppressive, as if an unseen weight pressed against the walls. Sharon began experiencing headaches whenever she lingered near the clock, as well as sharp pains that only eased when she left the room. Her visiting daughter complained of sudden dizziness and nausea.

The breaking point came late one night. Sharon had settled into her living room chair, attempting to watch a movie and distract herself from growing unease. But the oppressive atmosphere of the room made it hard to relax. Out of the corner of her eye, she noticed movement. It was subtle at first, but unmistakable.

The clock's pendulum, which had always swayed with a measured, gentle rhythm, was now swinging faster. Its motion was erratic, and far too rapid for a mechanism its size. She stared in disbelief, her breath catching in her throat as the pendulum's speed continued to increase. What happened next will be burned into her memory for the rest of her life.

Shaking, Sharon fled the room and locked herself into her bedroom for the rest of the night.

Desperate for help, Sharon reached out to us. Her email, sent in the early hours, was frantic and filled with fear. She had heard of our museum, and hoped that we could take the clock before it caused any more stress. Her only demand was urgency, as she refused to spend another night under the same roof as the sinister object.

When the clock arrived at the museum days later, it brought along with it an undeniable energy. As we are definitely no strangers to bizarre phenomena, we immediately noticed its peculiarities.

This is Case #080519, The Peculiar Pendulum. What began as an act of curiosity became a confrontation with the inexplicable, leaving those involved forever changed. A stark reminder of the unseen forces that sometimes attach themselves to the things we bring into our lives.

THE PARANORMAL ODDITIES
HAUNTED MUSEUM OF
 OF LEGENDS, SPOOKS AND ODDITIES

CASE FILE

NAME: THE PECULIAR PENDULUM

CASE#: 080522

DATE: August 5, 2022

CASE #: 080522 - The Peculiar Pendulum

CLIENT NAME: Sharon Brown
ALL OCCUPANTS AT LOCATION: Sharon (client), Dog
DATE OF CASE: July - August 2022
DATE CLIENT OBTAINED OBJECT: Saturday - July 27, 2022
CLIENT LOCATION: Massachusetts
LOCATION OBTAINED: Free on the side of the road
OBJECT MANUFACTURE ORIGIN: Unknown

POINT OF CONTACT
EMAIL SENT TO PARANORMAL COUPLE ACCOUNT:
From: **********@email.com
Date: August 5, 2022 at 4:07:21 AM EST
To: contact@paranormalcouple.com
Subject: I HAVE A HAUNTED OBJECT

Dear Satori and Cody,
My name is Sharon, and I need your help. I picked up a clock from the side of the road a week ago, and it has to go. Strange and terrifying things have been happening, and I'm afraid to keep it any longer. It's currently in my garage, but I want to send it to your museum as soon as possible. Please let me know how to proceed.
Thank you,
Sharon

PRELIMINARY PHONE INTERVIEW

PHONE INTERVIEW BY: Cody Ray DesBiens & Satori Hawes
DATE: Tuesday - August 6, 2022
CLIENT NAME: Sharon Brown
PHONE NUMBER: ***-***-****
EMAIL: ***********@email.com

DESCRIPTION OF OBJECT IN QUESTION:
- Large gingerbread style mantle clock made of wood.
- Tan in color with intricate carvings on the face.
- Large gold pointed pendulum behind a glass door.

HOW WAS THE OBJECT OBTAINED:
- Sharon states that she was driving home from work on July 27, 2022 when she noticed the clock sitting on the curb, near a trash bin.
- Believing that it was too beautiful to be discarded, she took it home.
- She states that she "cleaned it with some disinfectant wipes," and placed it on her fireplace mantle in the living room.
- The client felt no negative energy when she first brought the clock inside, but started to notice strange activity within hours.

WHY DO YOU THINK THE OBJECT IS THE CAUSE OF THE PARANORMAL ACTIVITY:
- The client states that the activity began the first night after bringing the clock home.
- The activity was small, but gradually became more obvious.
- She reports that every event that has occurred seemed directly tied to the clock's vicinity.
- She states that no other objects in the home have ever exhibited similar behavior.

HOW LONG HAVE YOU BEEN AT THIS LOCATION?:

- Sharon has lived in her home for six years.
- She expressed that she has never experienced any paranormal activity before obtaining the clock.
- Her home was built in the 1990s, and there is no known history of hauntings or deaths on the property.

UNEXPLAINED TEMPERATURE CHANGES:

- The client reported a significant drop in temperature in her living room while watching television a few days ago.
- She stated "I swore that I saw my own breath at one point, that's how cold it got!"
- She got up to check the thermostat, and to her surprise, it had read 70 degrees.
- She stated that the drop was localized to the area around the fireplace where the clock was displayed.
- Her daughter, who was visiting, also felt the mysterious chill, and described it as a "bone-deep cold."
- The major part of this claim is that the next room over was completely normal temperature wise.
- The other strange thing is that "less than a minute after checking the thermostat, the coldness went completely away. It felt like a warm rush entered the living room. It was a freaky experience."

UNEXPLAINED ANOMALIES WITH ELECTRICAL DEVICES:

- After the pendulum flew out of the clock, Sharon was locked in her bedroom. She claims that she could hear her television in the living room briefly turning off and on without explanation.
- The volume on the TV also seemed to be fluctuating as well.

UNEXPLAINED ILLNESS:

- Sharon reported experiencing headaches when sitting in her living room for extended periods.
- Her daughter complained of dizziness and nausea while in the living room, but felt fine in other areas of the house.
- At first, they did not think that this could be paranormal because nothing major had happened. This was before the pendulum experience.
- Sharon also noted that her dog avoided the living room entirely after the clock was introduced into the home.
- "At first, we thought the dog had seen a mouse or something and was frightened, we couldn't figure out why - but now it makes sense."

MANIPULATION OF OBJECTS:

- "The most unbelievable experience happened two nights ago."
- The client was watching TV in her living room, when out of the corner of her eye, she noticed something.
- The clock's pendulum began swinging at a much faster speed than it normally should.
- Sharon looked over in wonderment. Her first immediate thought was that "there must be some sort of an electrical malfunction happening."
- As she focused her eyes more on the pendulum, she realized that the direction of the pendulum's swing began to change from side-to-side, to front-to-back. This should not be mechanically possible for the clock's design.
- What happened next terrified the client so bad, that she was unable to sleep at all that night.
- The client states that the glass door on the clock swung open on its own, and that the pendulum "came flying out" towards her "like a spear." She states that it narrowly missed her leg.
- She then ran into her bedroom screaming.
- Client states that she locked the bedroom door, and stayed in there until the sun rose the next morning.

UNEXPLAINED ODORS:

- Once the sun came up the next morning, Sharon emerged from her room to find the clock still on the mantle. She states that the glass door was open, and the pendulum was still on the floor near her chair.
- Her first instinct was to get the clock out of the house. She put the pendulum back into the clock, and ran the item out to the garage to leave it in there.
- As she was moving the clock, the client reported a faint metallic smell that could not be traced to any source.
- As soon as the clock was in the garage, and the door was closed, the smell was no longer detected at all.

UNEXPLAINED SOUNDS:

- About an hour before the preliminary phone call, Sharon expressed that she had heard "ticking" coming from the living room.
- She states that there are no other clocks in that area of the house.
- She said it was only for a brief few seconds, but it was loud and clear enough to tell exactly what it was.
- She states "I'm not sure if the thing is getting in my head, or if I really heard the ticking."

UNEXPLAINED VOICES:

- None Reported

APPARITIONS/VISUAL ANOMALIES:

- None Reported

PHYSICAL CONTACT:

- The pendulum flying out of the clock narrowly missed the client's leg. It was a close call.
- She also describes feeling an intense pressure in her chest and shoulders when she would sit in her living room chair.
- Her dog also recoiled as though he was being touched during one of his attempts to enter the living room.
- "It seems like if something is with that clock, it definitely doesn't like dogs."

DESIRED RESULT / OUTCOME:

- Sharon wants the clock away from her home as soon as possible.
- She fears that the clock's energy could harm her, or anyone who visits her home if it remains in her possession.

INVESTIGATOR NOTES:

- We offered to drive to the client's home at our earliest convenience (this upcoming weekend) to pick up the clock, but she respectfully declined.
- Sharon stated that she appreciates the offer, but she wants the clock gone as soon as possible.
- She has requested to send the clock to the museum through the mail so it is gone from her property immediately.
- We have instructed the client where to send the package. We have also left her with some helpful steps and tips to ensure that when she is packing the clock, that the energy leaves with it.

NOTES:

DATE OF ENTRY TO MUSEUM: Friday - August 9, 2022

- The clock has arrived in the mail, and has been immediately placed within the quarantine room after reattaching the pendulum.
- Surprisingly, early observations reveal occasional minimal pendulum movements from side-to-side, despite the absence of power.
- After examining the clock closer, we have no explanation for this.
- We have placed the item on a small table in our quarantine room to continue to watch over it more closely.
- The pendulum has not moved for the past ten minutes since our examination, and placing the clock back onto the table.

CLIENT FOLLOW UP: Sunday - August 18, 2022 - PHONE CALL

- The client has reported feeling much lighter and at ease since the clock was removed from her home.
- Her daughter's headaches and dizziness have resolved, and the dog is no longer avoiding the living room.
- Sharon expressed immense gratitude, and stated that she will never pick up roadside items again.

IMPORTANT UPDATE: Tuesday - October 22, 2022

- Today, as Satori and I walked into the area of the museum where the clock is being stored, we noticed that the glass door was wide open.
- It is also important to note that the pendulum is still attached, and did not fall. We have no explanation as to why the door is open, especially to the degree in which it was open.
- We have closed the door, and repositioned the clock.
- No further updates at this time.

IMPORTANT UPDATE: Wednesday - April 12, 2023

- When we walked into the museum today, we once again found the glass door open.
- This time, the pendulum was on the floor in front of the clock.
- We have no rational explanation as to how this could've happened.
- Nothing else in the museum is out of place.

THE ETERNAL CLOCK

On the surface, it was just a clock. Oval shaped, with silver numbers and a brass frame. It had hung quietly on the living room wall for decades. Its ticking had once been a background rhythm to daily life, and a forgotten relic of an unhappy marriage. Judy Davis never liked the clock. She thought that it was an ugly thing, but she had left it up after her ex-husband Steve moved out in 2007. Steve had brought the clock into their home initially, and she thought that it had just seemed easier to leave it untouched rather than bother taking it down.

Years had passed by. The clock hung undisturbed, silent and unassuming. It was a part of the story of Judy's life, much like the man who had brought it into her home had been. And when news of his death came on May 15th, 2020, she hardly gave the old clock a second thought. That is, until it stopped.

It didn't just stop once, it stopped repeatedly. No matter how many times she replaced the batteries, or how often she adjusted it, the clock would always cease ticking at exactly 5:15 PM. That time is the exact date of Steve's death. At first, she brushed it off. Clocks break all the time, don't they? Perhaps it was old wiring, or a loose connection. Judy tried not to think too much about it, however, when the ticking began to echo faintly in other rooms, or cold drafts crept through her locked and shuttered home, or when whispers filled the silence of her nights, ignoring the clock was no longer an option.

The events escalated quickly. The sensation of light taps on her shoulder would startle Judy when she sat too close to the clock, as though someone was urging her to pay attention. Her other appliances around the house began to malfunction, as well. Clocks on other devices began blinking or unplugging themselves. Then there was the jab in the ribs, sharp and familiar. This was something that her ex-husband would do to tease her when they were together. It was as though he was standing right beside her again, mischievous and full of life, defying the boundaries of death itself.

Judy didn't really believe in ghosts, but Steve had always been a man of his word. One promise he had always joked about during their marriage began to echo in her mind: *"If I go before you, I'll haunt you. I'll find a way."*

By late May, she could no longer deny that he had found his way back to her. Whether it was through the clock, or something else, he was still there. His presence was lingering in every tap, every draft, and every unexplained sound. And the clock, his clock, seemed to be at the center of it all.

Desperate for help, Judy reached out to the museum. She didn't just want the clock gone, but all of the activity gone with it. *"I just want my house back."*

When we spoke with her, we uncovered more than we had anticipated. The clock wasn't just a random object, but a symbol of the time that Judy and Steve had shared. She had hated it from the moment she laid eyes on it, and he had always delighted in keeping it on the wall, as if to irritate her just a little. It was a memory, a reminder of all the little battles and compromises that had defined their relationship.

We had agreed to take the clock, but we warned her: removing the item might not be enough to end the disturbances. If her ex-husband is truly tied to her, he might find another way to make himself known. Still, she was insistent. The clock had to go.

When the box arrived at the museum, we unpacked the clock and placed it in our quarantine room for close observation.

For us, the real mystery was just beginning. What had tied the man so firmly to this particular clock? Was it the object itself, or something deeper. Could it be something unresolved in Steve's life, or hers? And what did the clock stopping at 5:15 PM, the exact time of his death, truly mean?

As we delved into the case of the Eternal Clock, we would confront questions about the nature of love, loss, and the thin veil between the living and the dead. Some bonds, we would discover, refuse to be broken even by death. And some promises last far longer than a lifetime.

This is Case #052720, The Eternal Clock.

CASE FILE

NAME: THE ETERNAL CLOCK

CASE#: 052720

DATE: May 27, 2020

CASE #: 052720 - The Eternal Clock

CLIENT NAME: Judy Davis
ALL OCCUPANTS AT LOCATION: Judy (Client)
DATE OF CASE: May 2020
DATE CLIENT OBTAINED OBJECT: Unknown
CLIENT LOCATION: Redmond, Washington
LOCATION OBTAINED: Unknown
OBJECT MANUFACTURE ORIGIN: Unknown

POINT OF CONTACT
EMAIL SENT TO PARANORMAL COUPLE ACCOUNT:
From: **********@email.com
Date: May 27, 2020, at 9:29 PM EST
To: contact@paranormalcouple.com
Subject: HAUNTED OBJECT
Hello,
My name is Judy and I'm reaching out because I believe I have an object that I should've thrown out years ago. This clock belonged to my ex-husband Steve, who passed away on May 15, 2020. Before his passing, he always jokingly promised that he would come back to haunt me. Since his passing, strange things have been happening. The clock stops at 5:15 PM, which is the day he died. There are also other unexplained occurrences around it.
Please let me know if you can help or if you would like to accept it as a donation.
Thank you,
Judy

PRELIMINARY PHONE INTERVIEW

PHONE INTERVIEW BY: Cody Ray DesBiens & Satori Hawes
DATE: Thursday - May 28, 2020
CLIENT NAME: Judy Davis
PHONE NUMBER: ***-***-****
EMAIL: **********@email.com

DESCRIPTION OF OBJECT IN QUESTION:

- Oval shaped vintage wall clock.
- Black background with a brass framed edge.
- Numbers are silver in color.
- Approximately 12 inches in length.

HOW WAS THE OBJECT OBTAINED:

- The clock originally belonged to Judy's ex-husband Steve.
- She does not remember where he had gotten it from, but vividly remembers when he hung it on their wall.
- She states that the only reason why she remembers that is because "when he was trying to hammer the nail in the wall, he kept missing the stud. So still, till this day, there are about five holes in the wall."
- She expressed that after the divorce, the clock was one of the few things that was left behind, "hanging on the wall where he left it."

WHY DO YOU THINK THE OBJECT IS THE CAUSE OF THE PARANORMAL ACTIVITY:

- The client states that there are two reasons that come to mind as to why she believes that the clock is haunted.
- The first reason is that the activity started immediately after Steve's death on May 15, 2020.
- The second reason is how the clock consistently stops at 5:15 PM. This is the exact date of his death.
- She states that it always stops at that exact time. "Never a minute before, or after."

- The client also expressed that she does not believe the clock is "possessed or anything," but believes that her ex-husband is using it to send some sort of message.
- "The dummy knew I would know it was him if he started playing with the clock. I always hated that thing from the first day he brought it home, and he knew it too. I thought it was ugly from day one, and I still hate it." -Judy

HOW LONG HAVE YOU BEEN AT THIS LOCATION?:
- Judy and Steve moved into the home in 1991.
- She states that they had gotten divorced in 2007. She remained living in the house, while he moved out.
- She also made it clear that the divorce was her decision, and that it was tough on her ex-husband. They remained friendly after the split, however.

UNEXPLAINED TEMPERATURE CHANGES:
- On the evening of May 15th, before the client knew of her ex-husband's passing, she was preparing for bed when she experienced a "cold draft blow into the living room where the clock is kept."
- This draft was unexplainable, as all windows and doors were completely shut and locked.
- She explains that the draft was "so different" and "memorable," that when she had heard of Steve's passing the next day, she immediately got chills and wondered if it was a visitation.

UNEXPLAINED ANOMALIES WITH ELECTRICAL DEVICES:
- The client states that the only odd electrical occurrence happened to other clocks she owned.
- For some odd reason, her bedroom alarm clock that resides on her nightstand came unplugged one day. This has never happened before.

- Also, the same morning that she discovered that strange incident, she also noticed that the clock on her microwave was now blinking. It seemed like it had come unplugged, as well, and she swiftly plugged it back in again.
- Judy expressed that she has taken these occurrences as a sign from her ex-husband to "pay more attention to his clock."

UNEXPLAINED ILLNESS:
- The client has reported an occasional "strange feeling."
- She states that this feeling is not of sickness or pain, but more of an "intuition that something is around."
- Judy describes it "being similar to the hair on your arm standing up when you get a cold chill."
- She explains that she usually gets this feeling right before something is about to happen.

MANIPULATION OF OBJECTS:
- As mentioned previously, the clock stops consistently at exactly 5:15 PM, regardless if Judy changes the battery out or not.
- She also states that she came home to the clock "crooked on the wall" a few days ago.

UNEXPLAINED ODORS:
- None Reported

UNEXPLAINED SOUNDS:
- Occasionally, the client hears faint "ticking sounds" emanating from other parts of the house. This occurs even when a clock isn't present in those rooms.
- Judy states that it sounds as if someone takes the clock off the wall, and walks around the house with it.
- "You can literally hear the ticking getting softer, and louder."

UNEXPLAINED VOICES:

- The client has heard what she describes as "soft whispers," though she cannot discern any words or a clear source.
- Judy describes that the only time she has heard these whispers, is when she hears the ticking moving around the house.
- "It's like he is walking around with the clock, talking to it! I don't get it, but it freaks me out!"

APPARITIONS/VISUAL ANOMALIES:

- None Reported.
- The client jokingly states, "Steve knows better than to show himself to me."

PHYSICAL CONTACT:

- Judy states that she has two main claims of paranormal activity that have been occurring repeatedly, as far as physical contact goes.
- The first is what she describes as a "light tap" on her shoulder that happens while sitting in the living room near the clock.
- When it first began, she initially thought that it was her imagination. After it happened, however, she looked around the room and noticed that the clock had stopped again at 5:15.
- Judy believes that when she feels the tap, it is because she hasn't given notice to the fact that the clock has been stopped.
- The other unexplainable activity that has occurred twice now is "a jab in the ribs."
- The client states that it is something he would do when they were still together, and that it would always make her "jump."

DESIRED RESULT / OUTCOME:

- Judy wishes to donate the clock to the museum, fearing that the activity will continue if she doesn't.
- She states that she has already removed it from the wall, and is ready to ship it to us.

INVESTIGATOR NOTES:

- Steve frequently joked that he would "haunt her" after his passing.
- The consistent stopping of the clock at 5:15PM suggests that this could be related to Steve. He could possibly be trying to follow through with his promise.
- We believe the object may just be a random item he chose to use in order to get the client's attention.
- We have warned Judy that donating the clock most likely won't make her ex-husband go away.
- She still insists that she wants it gone.
- Satori and I have instructed Judy on how to set ground rules in order to have control over her home, just in case donating the clock doesn't stop the activity.

OTHER NOTES:

- We have instructed the client on where, and how to ship the clock to the museum.
- The clock will be placed within the quarantine room for observation once it arrives, before being added to the main collection.

NOTES:

DATE OF ENTRY TO MUSEUM: Wednesday - June 3, 2020

- The clock was received today by mail.
- Satori and I have placed it within the quarantine room for monitoring.
- We have also placed a digital voice recorder next to the clock in order to closely listen for any volume fluctuation with the ticking sound.

CLIENT FOLLOW UP: Friday - June 12, 2020 - PHONE CALL

- Judy reports feeling a significant sense of relief since the clock was removed from her home.
- She states that she still has an odd occurrence periodically, but nothing compared to when the clock was still in the home.
- Judy also expressed that she has set ground rules, and believes that it substantially helped diminish the amount of activity.

IMPORTANT UPDATE: Thursday - July 14, 2022

- Today, we found the clock laying down off of its stand.
- At first, we thought that it may have slid off. After we tried to recreate the movement, however, we found that the clock would have had to lift itself off of a small lip (on the stand we have for it) to slide off.
- This is the first time we have witnessed something strange with this item.

SETTING GROUND RULES

Living in a haunted house can be unsettling, but establishing ground rules with spirits is a strong way to set boundaries, and regain a sense of control. This is what we tell our clients to try:

1. Acknowledge Their Presence

Start by calmly recognizing the spirits. You can say something like, "I know you're here, and I respect your presence." This lets the spirits know that you are aware of them, which can help ease any possible tension.

2. Set Clear Boundaries

Verbally state with confidence what behavior is acceptable, and what isn't. For example: "You're welcome to stay, but please do not scare me, or others. Do not touch anyone, or disrupt daily activities."

3. Perform a Cleansing Ritual

Depending on your beliefs, use appropriate herbs, incense, or prayer to cleanse your space, while stating your intentions out loud.

4. Stay Consistent

If your boundaries are violated, reinforce them immediately. Repeat your rules with more authority.

SECONDHAND SPIRITS:

GHOSTLY OBJECTS FROM ESTATE SALES AND THRIFT STORES

OBJECTS FROM SECOND HAND STORES

* Rich Histories: Items often come from long, varied lives, carrying the energy of their previous owners.

* Emotional Attachments: Objects tied to significant events or memories may retain lingering emotions.

* Unresolved Energies: Items from tragic or untimely deaths may hold unsettled spirits.

* Spiritual Practices: Some items, like mirrors or jewelry, may have been used in rituals, or hold symbolic power.

FUN FACT:
The first time that we ever investigated together was at an antique store in Connecticut.

There is a certain kind of thrill to browsing estate sales and thrift stores—the promise of finding hidden treasures, unique items with history, and remnants of lives lived long before us. For many, these pieces are simply vintage finds or curiosities. But what happens when one of these objects brings home more than just nostalgia? What if, hidden beneath these items, there lurks a lingering presence, spirit, or a trace of something unseen? Next, we explore the world of haunted objects that have found new homes through estate sales and thrift stores. We will cover cases where seekers of both bargains and history have unwittingly brought home spirits of the past.

When someone passes away, their cherished possessions often find their way into estate sales or thrift stores, becoming part of a cycle of secondhand goods. But what happens when an item was more than just an everyday possession—when it symbolized a deep emotional connection for its owner? For some spirits, letting go of such an item might not come so easily. Their attachment to the object could transcend death, creating a link between their energy, and the material world. When that object is purchased by a new owner, it may draw the spirit's attention, sometimes in unsettling ways.

When these items end up in unfamiliar hands, the spirit of their former owner may feel compelled to "check up" on their prized possession. In some cases, this connection can manifest as harmless phenomena: flickering lights, an unexplained chill, or the sense of being watched. But not all spirits are passive observers. If the new owner treats that item with neglect, or if the spirit simply resents the item's presence in a new home, the energy tied to the object can shift into something darker.

Reports of havoc caused by secondhand objects are surprisingly common. Buyers have experienced strange occurrences such as doors slamming shut, disturbing sounds in the dead of night, or even an overwhelming sense of dread or anger tied to the item. In extreme cases, a spirit may escalate their activity to make their dissatisfaction clear. Items may be moved or thrown, electrical devices may malfunction, or the new owner may experience bouts of inexplicable "bad luck." These disturbances often seem to stop once the problematic item is returned, sold, or donated elsewhere. This shows that the spirit's attachment was less to the living person or location, and more to the object itself.

This raises an unsettling question: what happens when you unknowingly acquire a treasured possession? Could a spirit be drawn back to ensure that the item is treated with the same care it once received from its previous owner? Or might the spirit be always present, and simply reject the idea of their beloved object belonging to a stranger? Whatever the answer, these next stories offer a chilling reminder that some objects come with more than a price tag—they carry the lingering echoes of the past, and sometimes, those echoes demand to be heard.

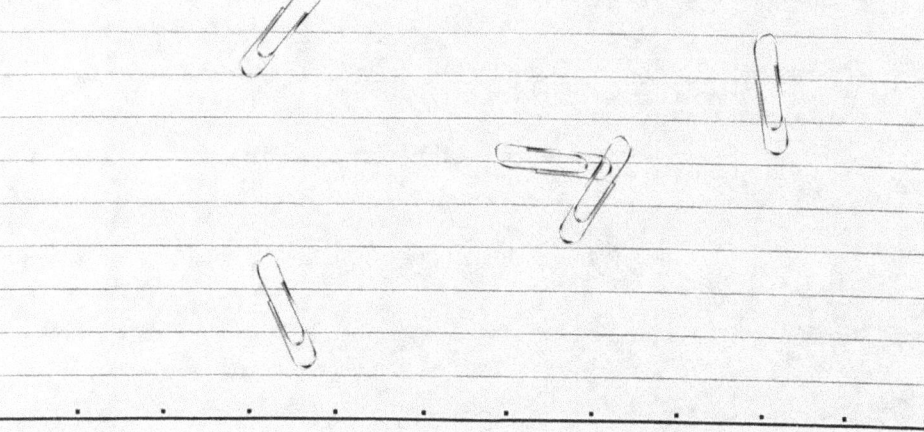

THE PIVOTAL PUPPETS

In February of 2020, a woman named Jane Clark of North Scituate, Rhode Island, contacted the museum seeking help for an unsettling situation. Jane had never experienced anything paranormal over the years spent in her home, that is, until she purchased two vintage hand puppets.

On February 16, 2020, Jane had wandered into a local Rhode Island thrift store. Her eyes were scanning the shelves of long forgotten trinkets in the hopes of finding something that she may enjoy in her own home. She wasn't looking for anything in particular, yet a pair of puppets caught her attention immediately.

The puppets, plastic headed figures with simple cloth bottoms, were the kind of find that most would dismiss as harmless, or even playful. But for Jane, these puppets would become a source of escalating fear. Intensely drawn to what she believed to be nothing more than their dated charm at the time, she brought the puppets home to her apartment. By doing this, she unknowingly invited an unexplainable presence into her life.

Almost immediately, Jane noticed a change in the atmosphere of her living space. What had always been a quiet, comfortable place, now felt crowded and abnormal. The odd occurrences began subtly: electronic door locks malfunctioning, lights turning on by themselves, and faint shuffling noises in the night. At first, Jane brushed off these incidents, chalking them up to coincidence, or human error. Over the next week, however, the peculiarities multiplied. With the activity growing, so did Jane's concern.

But everything came to a head on February 28th, 2020. Returning home from a trip to the supermarket, the first anomaly greeted Jane as she entered her residence. She noticed that three lights were mysteriously turned on. These lights are the very ones she would usually turn on herself when arriving home. Setting the groceries aside, she rationalized the lights as a coincidence, though the explanation felt thin.

Then, she began to hear strange shuffling noises coming from her bedroom. Was somebody else in her apartment?

Her heart raced as she quietly walked down the hallway, dread building up inside her with each step. When she found the source of the sounds, she was horrified by what she saw. What she encountered on the other side of her bedroom door would change her life, and her beliefs, forever.

The puppets were moving. Not just shifting slightly, but full on moving. It was as if they had come to life.

Frozen in shock, Jane watched in terror until a scream finally escaped her lips. The puppets instantly fell limp, collapsing onto their wooden stand. Summoning all her courage, Jane approached them with a plastic ruler from her desk, and began poking the figures to ensure that they were lifeless. The stillness only deepened her confusion and fear.

Within minutes, Jane fled the room, grabbing her laptop on her way out to compose the email that would lead her to us.

The email arrived to our museum on an uneventful evening, cutting through the dullness of daily life with an urgent plea for help. Its subject line, "PLEASE HELP ME," conveyed a raw desperation. The sender was not your typical client. She lived alone in a modest two bedroom apartment, and had never experienced anything that she would describe as supernatural before. She was the only experiencer of the activity, and was truly longing for someone else to listen and believe her.

When we first spoke with Jane that same evening, her words painted a vivid picture of a home turned upside down. Beyond the puppets' inexplicable movements, Jane admitted that she had begun noticing other odd occurrences in hindsight. Faint voices that seemed closer than they should have, shuffling sounds from her bedroom at night, and even the sensation of walking through cobwebs in open spaces. These eerie details, coupled with the puppets' bizarre behavior, convinced her that her once tranquil home had been invaded by something supernatural.

Jane was certain on one thing, she wanted the puppets gone. While she appreciated the harmless nature of some incidents, she no longer felt safe in her own home.

The case of The Pivotal Puppets stands as a reminder of how ordinary vintage objects can carry extraordinary energy from the hands that they have passed through. While Jane's experience was unsettling, her courage to confront the unknown and seek help ensured her home was restored to peace. Now, housed safely within our museum, the puppets remain under observation. Their mysterious nature is being carefully observed, and documented. Whether their activity was the product of a restless spirit, a form of residual energy, or something beyond our current understanding, these puppets serve as a compelling artifact in the ongoing exploration of the paranormal. For Jane, the experience may be behind her. For the puppets, however, their story has only just begun.

This is Case #022820, The Pivotal Puppets.

CASE FILE

NAME: THE PIVOTAL PUPPETS

CASE#: 022820

DATE: February 28, 2020

CASE #: 022820 - The Pivotal Puppets

CLIENT NAME: Jane Clark
ALL OCCUPANTS AT LOCATION: Jane (Client)
DATE OF CASE: February / March 2020
DATE CLIENT OBTAINED OBJECT: February 16, 2020
CLIENT LOCATION: North Scituate, Rhode Island
LOCATION OBTAINED: A Thrift Store
OBJECT MANUFACTURE ORIGIN: Unknown at this time

POINT OF CONTACT
EMAIL SENT TO PARANORMAL COUPLE ACCOUNT:
From: *********@email.com
Date: February 28, 2020 at 5:07:21 PM EST
To: contact@paranormalcouple.com
Subject: PLEASE HELP ME

I am looking for someone to talk to about the 2 puppets I have. I have
never seen anything like what I just saw and im not sure what to do
about it. Please call or email me as soon as you can. I live alone and I am
scared. Please don't think I'm crazy.
Thank you,

Jane
--****

PRELIMINARY PHONE INTERVIEW

PHONE INTERVIEW BY: Cody Ray DesBiens & Satori Hawes
DATE: Friday - February 28, 2020
CLIENT NAME: Jane Clark
PHONE NUMBER: ***-***-****
EMAIL: *********@email.com

DESCRIPTION OF OBJECT IN QUESTION:
- Two vintage hand puppets.
- Plastic heads and cloth bodies.

HOW WAS THE OBJECT OBTAINED:
- The client purchased the two puppets at a local thrift store.
- She states that the purchase was very "compulsive" because when she first locked eyes with the items, she immediately thought that they had a "retro vibe," and would look great in her bedroom.

WHY DO YOU THINK THE OBJECT IS THE CAUSE OF THE PARANORMAL ACTIVITY:
- Jane has had the puppets for a little over a week now. Ever since they had first been introduced into her apartment, the "feeling has been off."
- She states that she couldn't quite comprehend what was causing her space to feel that way, but after the events that happened tonight, she fully knows why.
- It is also important to note that Jane has never experienced anything paranormal at this location before.
- She states that the "off feeling" wasn't bad, just "different."

HOW LONG HAVE YOU BEEN AT THIS LOCATION?:
- Jane has lived at this location, alone, for the past 7 years.
- She states that her home space has always felt "normal" until the puppets were brought in.
- Once they came into the building, it always felt like there were multiple people there now.
- She states that "it feels like you are walking into a crowded room."

UNEXPLAINED TEMPERATURE CHANGES:

- None Reported.

UNEXPLAINED ANOMALIES WITH ELECTRICAL DEVICES:

- Jane states that her electronic door locks have been malfunctioning over the past week or so.
- She states that she will lock the door when she leaves, and later come home to find the door unlocked.
- This is something that has never happened before.
- She also states that sometimes, she will come home to the lights already on inside her apartment. The interesting thing is that everytime she comes home, she always turns on the same three lights as her routine.
- Jane explains that those three lights are the same ones that get turned on by themselves, "almost like the spirit has been watching."
- She states that she does not feel threatened by this phenomenon. She actually appreciates it.

UNEXPLAINED ILLNESS:

- None Reported.

MANIPULATION OF OBJECTS:

- The manipulation of the two puppets is the reason why Jane contacted the museum.
- This evening, when the client arrived home from visiting the supermarket, the three lights were turned on.
- After putting her groceries away, she heard noise coming from her bedroom. When she went to investigate, she was blown away.
- Jane states that "it was like a scene out of the Toy Story movies."
- She expressed that "the two puppets were dancing, as if a hand was inside of them."
- She said that these dolls were "moving their hands and head. They were interacting with each other like they were alive!"

- As soon as Jane screamed, the puppets went limp and dropped back onto their stands.
- After composing herself, she approached the puppets, and poked them with a ruler she had found on her desk. Her hope was to clear the thought that something living could be inside of them.
- After confirming that nothing was inside of them, she grabbed her laptop and left the bedroom to email our museum.

UNEXPLAINED ODORS:
- None Reported.

UNEXPLAINED SOUNDS:
- Jane explains that over the last week and a half, she has heard similar shuffling noises coming from her bedroom. She never suspected that it could be the puppets moving.
- Client states that after seeing the puppets move, she has begun to realize all of the "odd occurrences" that she chalked up to normal reasoning.
- She now suspects that the puppets have moved more than the one time she had witnessed it with her own eyes.
- Jane now believes that every time she has heard those shuffling sounds, that it was the result of the puppets actually moving.

UNEXPLAINED VOICES:
- The client states that unexplained voices are another occurrence that she has heard over the past week, but did not consider it paranormal at the time.
- She just assumed that someone was walking outside, and talking loudly.
- Jane now states that looking back, the voice sounded much closer and clearer than it should have been if a living person was walking by, and talking.
- The client does not remember what was being said, because she wasn't paying close attention to it.

APPARITIONS/VISUAL ANOMALIES:
- None Reported.

PHYSICAL CONTACT:
- Jane expresses that over the past few days, she has had the feeling of "walking through spiderwebs."
- She states that the odd thing about this occurrence is that she would feel this sensation in spots of the home where spiderwebs shouldn't be, (such as the center of a room.)

OTHER NOTES:
- The client states that she is not overly traumatized by tonight's experience, but no longer wants the puppets in her home.
- She says that "the experience was more startling than scary."
- Satori and I have also confirmed that Jane has no pets, therefore, there are no living factors that could have accidentally moved the puppets. (This explanation seems very unlikely even if she did have a pet.)

DESIRED RESULT / OUTCOME:
- Jane has made it very clear that she appreciates the spirit turning on the lights for her, but does not want the puppets in her apartment anymore.
- She now wants to donate the puppets to the museum to "give them a nice home."

INVESTIGATOR NOTES:
- Satori and I plan to pick up the puppets in-person at a public location (at Jane's request.)
- The scheduled meetup is on Sunday - March 1, 2020, at a local mall parking lot.

IN-PERSON VISIT / OBJECT PICKUP

DATE OF VISIT: Sunday - March 1, 2020
INVESTIGATORS PRESENT: Cody Ray DesBiens & Satori Hawes
LOCATION RESIDENTS PRESENT: Jane (Client)

PRELIMINARY NOTES UPON ARRIVAL:

- When Satori and I arrived at the meeting spot, we were immediately greeted by Jane.
- She seemed very kind, and was excited to pass the puppets on to their new home.
- We also asked her if anything unusual happened last night, and she stated that nothing had happened.
- We have instructed her to contact us if anything paranormal continues to occur at her home now that the objects have been removed.

NOTES:

DATE OF ENTRY TO MUSEUM: Sunday - March 1, 2020

- Today, Satori and I placed the puppets within the quarantine room to observe them for the next couple of weeks.
- The puppets came to us on a wooden stand that we have continued to leave them on.

CLIENT FOLLOW UP: Saturday - March 14, 2020 - PHONE CALL

- Satori & myself were able to reach Jane over the phone.
- She stated that everything has been going great, and she has had no more incidents with her door lock, or lights.
- Jane also stated that she has not heard any other strange noises coming from her bedroom.
- Even though part of her misses these interactions, she is happy that the puppets "are in a better home."

IMPORTANT UPDATE: Monday - January 4, 2021

- This evening when I (Cody) entered the museum, I found one of the puppets (the puppet with blue clothing) lifted halfway off of its stand. It's head was hanging, slumped over, off of its stand.
- I can not find any normal explanation as to how this could have happened.
- The other puppet looks to have not moved at all.

IMPORTANT UPDATE: Friday - February 16, 2024

- When we entered the museum today, we began to dust the shelves. While doing this, we found that the two puppets were both spun around, facing the wall behind them.
- We are now rearranging some of our newest item additions around this section, to see if this affects the energy surrounding the puppets.

THE MEL METER

The Mel Meter's main function is to detect potential paranormal activity by measuring electromagnetic fields (EMF) and temperature fluctuations simultaneously. It was designed by Gary Galka, an engineer, after the tragic loss of his daughter, Melissa ("Mel"). He created it as a way to communicate with spirits, and honor her memory.
The device's features include:

EMF Detection:
Measures electromagnetic fields, which are believed to be associated with paranormal activity.

Temperature Sensor:
Monitors sudden temperature changes that may occur during paranormal events.

Additional Features:
Certain versions also include additional functions like a REM (Radiating EM Field) detector, and a Shadow Detection circuit.

The Mel Meter is widely used by investigators due to its precision and dual-functionality, making it a staple for those exploring the paranormal.

CLOWN CHAOS

Some objects seem destined to disrupt the balance of ordinary life, even when they appear harmless or, in this case, harmlessly creepy. For Maria Lewis and her family in Valley City, North Dakota, what began as a routine thrift-store outing in early 2022, turned into an unsettling chapter in their lives. Their modest haul of vintage finds included an interesting 8-inch clown doll with a plastic head, and cloth body. At first, it seemed like nothing more than a quirky, creepy addition to their basement entertainment room. The doll's arrival, however, ended up marking the beginning of a peculiar series of events. Events that would end up leaving this family shaken, and desperate for answers.

Maria could still remember the moment that she had first seen it. The doll sat on a low shelf near the entrance of the thrift store, its weighted body sagging in an almost lifelike way. Its painted-on grin frozen in an unsettling smirk. Something about the clown made her stomach tighten, but she kept silent. Her family, as usual, had scattered throughout the store in search of hidden treasures, leaving Maria alone with her unease.

By the time that they had regrouped to check out, Maria was the only one without something in her hands. This was truly a rare occurrence. Her eldest son Austin, however, proudly clutched the very same clown doll that had caught her attention earlier. "Really?" she asked, raising an eyebrow. "Of all the things in this store?"

Austin just looked at her and shrugged. "It's creepy. I like it." His younger brother Tyler grinned in agreement, already imagining how the doll might serve as the perfect prop for their future pranks.

Maria's husband just laughed, and patted Austin's shoulder. "Let the boys have their fun," he said, oblivious to the chill that ran through his wife as the clown was added to their pile of purchases.

At first, the doll's role in the family was barely more than an inside joke. The boys had placed it on a shelf in the basement. This was where it oversaw all of their movie nights, and video game sessions. Its eerie grin became the source of occasional jabs and dares, but the humor quickly soured.

Maria was the first to notice the change. The house felt heavier, as though its familiar warmth had been replaced by something dense, and oppressive. The air seemed to carry an invisible weight, and soon, everyone began feeling it. Arguments began to break out over trivial things. Nights grew restless, and the once cozy home now felt cold, and foreign.

Still, no one connected these changes to the clown. This was the case, however, until the disturbances became impossible to ignore.

It started with faint movements, or so the family thought. Whenever they entered the basement, one of the boys would swear the doll had shifted its position. At first, the accusations were dismissed as terrible pranks, each sibling trying to out-scare the other. But Maria couldn't shake her unease.

Then, one night, a deafening crash shattered the silence. The family bolted out of bed, racing downstairs only to find their two large bookcases toppled over. The damage should have buried the clown under a heap of books and trinkets, but to their horror, it sat perfectly upright. The doll was sitting atop one of the overturned shelves. Maria's husband whispered the thought that was on everyone's mind: "This doesn't make sense."
From that moment on, the disturbances escalated. Lights in the basement flickered erratically, odd smells would randomly waft throughout the entire house, all of it leaving the family bewildered.

Maria's mother Sandra, who lived with them, had her own unnerving encounter. One evening, she thought that she saw Austin pass by her doorway. When she called out to him, however, there was no response. She went to investigate, only to find the hallway empty.

By March, Maria had reached her breaking point. The clown, once a harmless curiosity, had become a source of nothing but dread. The next step was to contact the museum. Maria hoped to remove the doll from her home, and with it, the disturbances that had upended her family's lives.

But even after the clown was safely sent away, its strange influence continued to leave its mark.

This is Case #031022, Clown Chaos. A stark reminder that some objects carry far more than what meets the eye. Even the smallest, most unassuming objects, can harbor something far beyond the ordinary.

CASE FILE

NAME: CLOWN CHAOS

CASE#: 031022

DATE: March 10, 2022

CASE #: 031022 - Clown Chaos

CLIENT NAME: Maria Lewis
ALL OCCUPANTS AT LOCATION: Maria (client), Husband James, Son Austin (17), Son Tyler (14), Grandmother Sandra (Maria's mother)
DATE OF CASE: February & March of 2022
DATE CLIENT OBTAINED OBJECT: February 12 or 13 of 2022
CLIENT LOCATION: Valley City, North Dakota
LOCATION OBTAINED: Thrift Store
OBJECT MANUFACTURE ORIGIN: Unknown / No Makers Mark

POINT OF CONTACT
EMAIL SENT TO PARANORMAL COUPLE ACCOUNT:
From: ***********@email.com
Date: March 10, 2022 at 11:40:51 PM EST
To: WEBSITE - contact@paranormalcouple.com
Subject: I Have A Haunted Object

Hello, is there an address to send a possessed thing to? We would like some assistance or at least your opinion on what to do if possible. Thank you,

Maria

PRELIMINARY PHONE INTERVIEW

PHONE INTERVIEW BY: Cody Ray DesBiens & Satori Hawes
DATE: Saturday - March 12, 2022
CLIENT NAME: Maria Lewis
PHONE NUMBER: ***-***-****
EMAIL: ***********@email.com

DESCRIPTION OF OBJECT IN QUESTION:

- Weighted, sitting clown.
- Made with a cloth body and plastic head.
- Approximately 8 inches in length.

HOW WAS THE OBJECT OBTAINED:

- Every few months or so, the client and her family (husband and two children) go to a local thrift store to look for "fun and interesting things."
- Maria stated that they usually walk away with some "vintage clothes, books, or a few vinyl records." She also states that she has been shopping at this store more than a dozen times, but something felt different about this last visit.
- She then expressed that when she first walked through the front door of the store, the clown was the first thing that she had locked eyes with. She states that she immediately got an "off feeling" about the clown, but felt no need to say anything.
- All of the family members split up in the store to look around, as was usual. Approximately 20 or 30 minutes later, everyone joined back up in the middle of the store to check out. All but one family member was empty handed, which was very unusual.
- The client's 17 year old son, Austin, had picked up the clown that she had locked eyes with when they first arrived at the store.
- She questioned Austin on why he had picked that "thing" out of everything in the store, and his response was that he and his brother thought that it "looked creepy."
- Much to the client's dismay, her husband helped the boys check out, and paid for the clown. They then became the proud new owners of something that "looked creepy."

HOW LONG HAVE YOU BEEN AT THIS LOCATION?:

- Maria and James purchased their home in 2006.
- Client states that an addition was built onto the home in 2011 to make room for her mother, Sandra, to move in.
- The reason why Sandra moved in with the family was because her husband had unfortunately passed away, and she no longer wanted to live alone.

WHY DO YOU THINK THE OBJECT IS THE CAUSE OF THE PARANORMAL ACTIVITY:

- Maria states that ever since she first locked eyes with the clown, everything has seemed "heavy and off," especially now that it is under the same roof as her.
- She states that she (and the family) had never experienced anything paranormal before, until the clown was brought into the home.
- She said "major things started happening with no explanation..."

MANIPULATION OF OBJECTS:

- "YES!"
- Maria states that when the clown was brought home, her sons had placed it on one of the bookcase shelves in the basement. This is where the family entertainment room is.
- At first, when they would go downstairs to watch TV, one family member would occasionally express that the clown had looked as if it had "moved slightly" since the last time they had seen it.
- The client states that no one ever knew if it was really happening, or if the kids were just trying to scare each other. She says that it was all "questionable, until a couple of nights ago."
- This past weekend, Maria and her family were all upstairs when a "house shaking boom" came from the basement.
- The client states that she and James then rushed downstairs to see what had happened, and when they got there, were in total disbelief and shock.

- They discovered that the bookcase in which the clown was sitting, as well as another bookcase about 15 feet away, had both fallen forward to the ground at the same time. There was no logical explanation.
- What's even more intriguing is how the client (and family) discovered the clown. It was sitting perfectly upright, situated on top of the upside down bookcase; like he had been placed there.
- This did not make sense to the client, or her family, because the clown should've been buried under the mess.

UNEXPLAINED ODORS:
- At first, Maria was surprised by this question.
- She states that she, and the rest of the family, have experienced the smell of a "race track, like burning rubber" approximately 4 times over the past few weeks.
- The reason why she was surprised by this question was because she had never expected the object to be the cause of the smell.
- She stated that "it all makes sense now. It didn't happen until the clown came into the house, but why would it smell like that?"
- We explained that residual smells are reported quite often, and the smell that is experienced could possibly be a smell that was important to the spirit.

UNEXPLAINED SOUNDS:
- Maria states that the only substantial sound was when the bookcases fell over.

UNEXPLAINED TEMPERATURE CHANGES:
- None Reported.

UNEXPLAINED ANOMALIES WITH ELECTRICAL DEVICES:
- This is another question that Maria was surprised by.
- She states that there have been "a few electrical problems," but did not think that the paranormal could be an explanation.

- She states that the basement lights are on a dimmer switch, and that the entire family has experienced the lights dim (almost completely off) on a few occasions.
- The lights have also flashed a few times, as well.
- She states that "it always seems like someone is trying to prank us."
- James has called an electrician to check on the light switches, and he is scheduled to come to the house in about a week.
- She states that she will update us after his assessment.

UNEXPLAINED ILLNESS:
- None Reported.

APPARITIONS/VISUAL ANOMALIES:
- The client's mother (Sandra) thought that the oldest grandchild (Austin) was coming to her room to say goodnight one evening.
- She was watching television in her room, when she claims that "a tall form walked past her doorway."
- She was waiting for him to come in, but it never happened. She got up to investigate, and stated that there was no one there.
- Sandra's room is the last room at the end of the hall. If it was a living person walking by, then there is no place for them to go once passing by her door.

UNEXPLAINED VOICES:
- The client recalls one instance in which her husband had scolded the kids for leaving the TV on in the basement.
- He, and the kids, all heard what sounded like the TV on. When they opened the basement door, however, the noise stopped instantly.
- The husband then ran downstairs to double check, and the TV was indeed off.

PHYSICAL CONTACT:
- None Reported.

DESIRED RESULT / OUTCOME:

- The client, and her family, are in agreement with sending the clown to the museum.
- She states that after the bookcases fell, her oldest son "no longer thinks the clown is cool."
- They all just want the house to "return to normal."

INVESTIGATOR NOTES:

- We instructed the client on where to send the clown.
- We also reminded her to update us after the electrician visits the home.

NOTES:

IMPORTANT UPDATE: Wednesday - March 16, 2022
EMAIL SENT TO PARANORMAL COUPLE ACCOUNT:
From: ***********@icloud.com
Date: March 16, 2022 at 5:32:08 PM EST
To: contact@paranormalcouple.com
Subject: Electrician Update

Hi Satori & Cody,

As promised, I wanted to send you an update. The electrician came out to our house today and did a full examination of the switches, wires, and breaker box and could not find one thing wrong. He said that he has no idea why the lights were doing that.
I personally believe that the clown was definitely responsible, but I didn't tell him that LOL.
Please let me know if the package arrives and if you guys experience anything. Thank you again for all of your help and assistance.

Maria Lewis

DATE OF ENTRY TO MUSEUM: Wednesday - March 18, 2022
- Today, Satori and I received the clown in a small box.
- We have placed the item within the quarantine room on top of a small bookshelf to establish a baseline.

CLIENT FOLLOW UP: Saturday - April 2, 2022 - PHONE CALL
- We were able to reach our client, Maria, over the phone.
- She states that "nothing weird has happened" since she sent the clown to us.
- She is very grateful that everything seems to be back to normal for them.

IMPORTANT UPDATE: Wednesday - July 13, 2022
- Upon entering the museum today, Satori and I noticed that the clown was now seated on a different shelf within the museum.
- It seems that he has moved down 2 shelf levels.
- Unfortunately, there are no cameras facing this direction.
- We have left the clown on its new shelf to see if it continues to move.
- Maybe the clown likes this shelf better.

IMPORTANT UPDATE: Saturday - August 5, 2023
- Today, while at an event, Satori and I had a selection of items from our museum on display, including the clown.
- At one point, a woman screamed and quickly left the room. She stated that she had seen the clown move on its own.
- We will be placing the clown back into the quarantine room for a week to observe it closer. We will do this once we return home.

IMPORTANT UPDATE: Saturday - September 2, 2023
- The clown has finished spending time within the quarantine room. Nothing abnormal has been documented.
- The object will now be moved back to its usual spot within the museum.

HORSE DRAWN SHADOWS

The allure of estate sales lies in the promise of uncovering forgotten treasures, as well as the potential for an item's second home and lifetime. For Lynn Johnson of Avon, Indiana, a seemingly normal Saturday detour to an estate sale, quickly turned into a journey that would forever alter her sense of reality. The sale was held at an old farmhouse Lynn had passed by and admired for years, a place that seemed submerged in nostalgia. On this particular day, Lynn felt an unusual pull to stop by. It was an inexplicable urge that she couldn't seem to shake. What awaited her inside was more than she could have imagined, a discovery that would end up leaving a lasting mark on her life.

Before Lynn had even stepped inside of the house, and encountered the item within this case file, paranormal activity was present to greet her. She had experienced an encounter so profound that it would likely remain etched into her memory, as well as the memory of others, for the rest of their lives. The only unfortunate part of this encounter was that she did not realize it was paranormal until the occurrence had already passed.

Once inside the farmhouse, the air within it felt heavy, as if weighed down by the secrets held within its walls. Among the various knickknacks and antiques, one item stood out: a small tin carousel. Its delicate craftsmanship and charm caught Lynn's eye immediately. Yet there was something peculiar about the carousel that set it apart from the other items. It had a small, hand-written note taped to its surface with the unsettling instruction, "Do not spin!" The warning seemed both bizarre, and intriguing, as if daring the finder to disobey. Intrigued but not overly concerned, Lynn purchased the carousel, brushing off the note's ominous tone.

As she carried the carousel to her car, and endured a strange interaction with the new owner of the estate, an unshakable sensation crept over her. The feeling that grew was unfamiliar, and deeply unsettling. The feeling sent a chill racing down her spine, but she dismissed it as a product of her imagination, and some strange coincidences. Lynn was truly unaware that this moment only marked the beginning of something far more terrifying.

Once home, Lynn's curiosity got the best of her. What began as an interest quickly escalated into chilling encounters, as her home transformed from a loving sanctuary, into a stage for shadows and secrets. That night, she decided to spin the carousel, despite the note's warning. As the tin horses whirled around, and the quaint music box song filled the room, a cold bitterness quickly burst into the room. As the carousel slowed to a stop, an unnerving stillness seemed to settle over the house. The air continued to grow colder, and as Lynn backed away to get her husband Ray, she couldn't shake the feeling that she was no longer alone.

In the moments that followed, the atmosphere in Lynn's home took a sudden, and dramatic turn. A cascade of inexplicable and terrifying events unfolded, leaving Lynn and Ray paralyzed with fear, and consumed by complete hysteria.

Lynn reached out to us that night, and by the time we spoke on the phone, the carousel's influence had become undeniable. She recounted how that one spin seemed to summon something unseen— an energy that unleashed a spiritual mob around the perimeter of her home. She believed that this force was stalking her living space, and somehow filled it with an oppressive energy. While the Johnson's tried to make sense of what they had accidentally welcomed in, they became increasingly desperate for answers. The carousel, even with its seemingly beautiful music, remained silent on the subject of answers, offering no clues about its origins or the forces it seemed to call upon.

This is Case #061322, Horse Drawn Shadows. This case is a chilling tale of intuition, ignored warnings, and the unrelenting curiosity that bridges the worlds of the living, and the unknown. The unanswered questions linger still: Why was it marked with such a cryptic note? What forces stirred when it was spun? And most hauntingly, what price must be paid for venturing into the realm of the forbidden?

CASE FILE

NAME: HORSE DRAWN SHADOWS

CASE#: 061322

DATE: June 13, 2022

CASE #: 061322 - Horse Drawn Shadows

CLIENT NAME: Lynn Johnson
ALL OCCUPANTS AT LOCATION: Lynn (client), Husband Ray, Grandson Jason (15, periodically visits home)
DATE OF CASE: June 2022
DATE CLIENT OBTAINED OBJECT: Saturday - June 11, 2022
CLIENT LOCATION: Avon, Indiana
LOCATION OBTAINED: Estate Sale
OBJECT MANUFACTURE ORIGIN: Unknown

POINT OF CONTACT

EMAIL SENT TO PARANORMAL COUPLE ACCOUNT:
From: **********@email.com
Date: June 13, 2022 at 7:33:11 PM EST
To: contact@paranormalcouple.com
Subject: HAUNTED OBJECT

Dear Cody and Satori,
I hope this reaches you well. My name is Lynn and I have an item that I would like to get out of my home as soon as possible. I brought it home a few days ago from a local estate sale and things have not been going good at all here. I thought of you both immediately. Thank you and I hope to hear from you soon.

Lynn Johnson
Cell Phone Number: ***~***~****

PRELIMINARY PHONE INTERVIEW

PHONE INTERVIEW BY: Cody Ray DesBiens & Satori Hawes
DATE: Tuesday - June 14, 2022
CLIENT NAME: Lynn Johnson
PHONE NUMBER: ***-***-****
EMAIL: **********@email.com

DESCRIPTION OF OBJECT IN QUESTION:

- Small carousel, approximately 10 inches tall.
- Object is made out of a thin type of metal (tin or copper according to the client.)
- When the carousel is wound clockwise, the item begins to spin slowly, and play music.

HOW WAS THE OBJECT OBTAINED:

- It is important to note that for the past decade or so, Lynn has gotten a "curious feeling" whenever she would drive by a certain farm house. The property is about 30 minutes away from her home.
- Last weekend, she was driving by the house and noticed a large estate sale sign in the yard.
- At first, she passed by the home, but "something told her to turn around."
- Once Lynn exited her car, she was greeted by an elderly man who welcomed her to the property. The man explained to her that she could go inside the home and search around for anything that may interest her. He also told her that if she had "any questions," to ask his daughter inside.
- The client stated that there were 2 other people inside of the house, who were also browsing.
- She immediately got a strange feeling of paranoia when she entered, but she pushed through it.
- After looking around for a few minutes, Lynn states that she was "pulled" to an old shoebox on the bottom shelf of a bookcase.
- Upon opening the box, she found a metal carousel inside. On the item was a small note that read "do not spin!"
- Lynn was simply intrigued, and grabbed the box.

- As she was making her way to the front door with the box, she was stopped by a woman who asked if she needed any help.
- Lynn responded and asked about the carousel, but the woman did not have any information about it.
- After paying the woman for the item, she asked if her father outside would know anything more about it.
- The woman looked perplexed, and after a short pause, asked "what do you mean, father?"
- Lynn then explained that a man in overalls with white hair welcomed her to the property. She continued to explain that he had invited her in to look around, and told her that his daughter was inside if she had any questions.
- The woman responded that her father had actually passed away 2 weeks ago, which was why they were having the estate sale. Both of them began to freak out, especially the daughter after hearing that the man was wearing overalls. She stated that her father would wear them everyday.
- When they both ran outside, the man was gone. There was no one in sight.
- The client then drove home in shock, with the carousel in tow.

WHY DO YOU THINK THE OBJECT IS THE CAUSE OF THE PARANORMAL ACTIVITY:
- After experiencing her first paranormal encounter, she did not believe that the carousel had anything to do with it.
- It seemed like that experience was completely separate from what was to come.
- When the client initially brought the object into her home, she was feeling a sense of paranoia.
- She also began to wonder why the "do not spin!" note was on the item. Her first thought was that the carousel was broken, and that the note was to prevent someone from breaking it further. Her opinion on that would soon change...

- That night, she pulled the carousel out of the box and began to take a closer look at it. She had wondered if it was handmade, because there were no noticeable markings on it.
- Going against the note, the client placed the carousel on her table, and gave it a spin.
- As the music began to play, other paranormal activity began to happen...

HOW LONG HAVE YOU BEEN AT THIS LOCATION?:
- Lynn, and her husband Ray have lived in their home for approximately 20 years.
- She states that they had purchased the land and built the home themselves, so they are the first and only residents.

UNEXPLAINED TEMPERATURE CHANGES:
- When the carousel was spun, Lynn states that it immediately began "freezing" in the room that she was in.
- She expressed that the temperature had dropped within seconds, with no logical explanation.

UNEXPLAINED ANOMALIES WITH ELECTRICAL DEVICES:
- None Reported.

UNEXPLAINED ILLNESS:
- None Reported.

MANIPULATION OF OBJECTS:
- Once the carousel stopped spinning, Lynn got up from her chair to grab Ray.
- As she was backing away, she began to hear this "clicking sound," and noticed that the carousel was beginning to slowly wind itself up again.
- This made her scream, and move a lot quicker to the living room where her husband was.

UNEXPLAINED ODORS:
- None Reported.

UNEXPLAINED SOUNDS:
- While Lynn was explaining to Ray what she had just witnessed, the sound of the music box began to play from the other room.
- Both of them were now feeling extremely uneasy.
- They slowly approached the room containing the carousel, and watched as it came to a slow stop.
- Ray then approached the object, and placed it back into the shoebox.

UNEXPLAINED VOICES:
- None Reported.

APPARITIONS/VISUAL ANOMALIES:
- A few hours later, once Lynn and Ray had calmed down, they decided to take the carousel back out of the box.
- At this point, they thought that they were both going insane after what they had witnessed.
- Once it was sitting back on the table, Ray gave the top a good spin.
- Once the music started, a loud "pop sound" was heard in the house. This made them both start looking around the room for an explanation.
- The blinds were drawn on every window, and they were backlit by the porch lights.
- As they were glancing around, both Lynn and Ray were in absolute shock by what they saw.
- All of the outside windows had tall shadow figures walking by them. It looked as if they were circling the house.
- Lynn began screaming. Ray immediately threw the carousel back into its box, and kicked it across the room.
- As the music stopped, so did the shadows. They had now realized that whatever had just happened was triggered by the action of spinning the carousel.

PHYSICAL CONTACT:

- None Reported.

OTHER NOTES:

- One observation that Lynn made was that the mantle clock (located in the same room that the carousel was in) stopped working around the same time as the last paranormal experience.
- She states that it could just be a coincidence. She changed the battery, and it successfully started back up again.

DESIRED RESULT / OUTCOME:

- Lynn and Ray want the carousel gone as soon as possible, before their 15 year old grandson, Jason, comes over to visit.
- They stated that they were originally going to bring it back to the farmhouse. It soon occurred to them that the owner must've experienced something paranormal, as well. This is why they believe that the note was placed on the item. They doubted that the object would be accepted back, because of this reason.
- They now believe that the note was a warning to whoever came across the carousel, after the old man passed away.

INVESTIGATOR NOTES:

- We instructed Lynn on where to send the object, and what to do once the item has left their home.
- The unfortunate thing about the carousel is that we will never know its true backstory.

NOTES:

DATE OF ENTRY TO MUSEUM: Monday - June 20, 2022

- Today, Satori and I received a box containing the carousel.
- Upon opening the box, I (Cody) got an "unusual feeling."
- We immediately placed the item in quarantine for observation.

CLIENT FOLLOW UP: Friday - July 8, 2022 - PHONE CALL

- We were able to reach our client, Lynn, over the phone.
- She stated that no other abnormal events have occurred since the carousel has left the home.
- She asked us if we had spun the carousel yet, and we told her that we had not.
- She assured us to "brace yourselves when you are ready to do it."

IMPORTANT UPDATE: Tuesday - July 19, 2022

- Today, something strange happened as we were entering the museum.
- As we were walking through the door, we heard the ending notes of the music box song.
- The item just came out of quarantine a few days ago, and was sitting on our case file photo table.
- I (Cody) have a strange feeling that there is more to come with this item.

IMPORTANT UPDATE: Saturday - September 9, 2023

- Over the last six months or so, we have heard the carousel music multiple times, without ever touching it.
- We continue to document its activity in the hopes of learning more about it.

THE FACES OF FEAR:

HAUNTED MASKS

MASKS

✳ **Ritual Use:** Masks used in rituals or ceremonies are believed to absorb spiritual energy, particularly if they are used for summoning spirits, honoring deities, or exorcisms.

✳ **Ancestral Spirits:** In some cultures, masks are thought to house the spirits of ancestors or inhuman entities, which could linger and create a haunting presence.

✳ **Sacrificial Ties:** Masks used during sacrificial rites may be ingrained with the energy of the life taken, leading to ghostly activity.

FUN FACT:
One of our "Top Five" most haunted items happens to be an African mask donated from New Orleans.

Within countless cultures across the globe, masks have long been held with profound significance. Numerous cultures view masks as more than decorative objects; they are viewed as spiritual portals, vessels, and shields. Hand-carved masks often carry the essence of the people who created them, the rituals they were used in, and the emotions or entities they were meant to evoke. Over centuries, many of these masks have taken on a reputation—not merely as artifacts of history, but as haunted relics, brimming with energy.

Masks hold a unique power due to their design, and purpose to transform. In many cultures, masks can grant its wearer the identity of a warrior, a god, an elemental, a serviceable spirit, or even a demon. This transformative nature creates a psychic resonance—a blending of human intent, spiritual purpose, and sometimes, supernatural consequence. Ritual masks from Africa, Asia, the Americas, and Oceania were, and sometimes still are, used in ceremonies to summon spirits, honor ancestors on the other side, or ward off malevolent forces. Yet, in channeling these energies, the masks can sometimes become anchors for spirits, residual emotions, or lingering power.

Many supposed haunted masks are said to carry imprints of the rituals they were part of: the fervent chants of shamans, the powerful dances of initiates, or the silent prayers of those seeking health and protection. When a mask is worn, it becomes a bridge between the physical and spiritual realms. If not properly consecrated or cared for after its use, the energies that the mask was exposed to may linger. That energy may manifest in ways that inspire both in awe, and terror, within the inexperienced individuals that it comes into contact with.

Collectors and historians alike recount chilling tales of masks that seem to come alive—shifting positions, exuding cold air, or emanating whispers in empty rooms. Some claim that the spirits bound to haunted masks are all protective, while others believe that there are some that are not so benevolent.

Not all haunted masks come from sacred rituals, or ancient traditions. Some are tourist souvenirs, simply carved and mass-produced to embody the cultural aesthetics of faraway lands. Yet even these masks can carry paranormal energy. Many are created to mimic traditional designs and art forms, but lack the spiritual intent of their original counterparts. Despite this, the act of mimicking sacred or ceremonial art is theorized by some to draw attention from restless spirits or powerful energies. Creating masks, even for tourism purposes, is a form of labor and love from the artist, as well. Some believe that the artist may, one day, find themselves checking-in on their beloved work in spirit. This could also be a cause of paranormal activity among tourist art pieces.

In other cases, there are masks that are oftentimes sold to tourists that were once part of genuine rituals. These masks were exported from their original homeland without proper cultural education among new owners. This careless displacement can potentially anger spirits that are attached to haunted masks, causing them to become conduits for strange occurrences in the homes of unsuspecting buyers. Tales abound of tourists who have brought home decorative masks, only to experience unsettling phenomena such as unexplained shadows, disembodied voices, or an overwhelming sense of being watched. These stories serve as a cautionary reminder: even the seemingly harmless can hold untold power.

Up next, we explore some of our more unusual cases of haunted masks, diving into the mysterious phenomena they evoke. These faces, carved in wood, tell stories of devotion, fear, power, and the eternal interplay between the seen and unseen. When you gaze into their hollow eyes, do not be surprised if someone, or something, stares back.

MASKS WITH SPIRITUAL INFLUENCE DONATED TO THE MUSEUM

Ghost Mask • Côte d'Ivoire • Liberia

GHOST MASK

PURPOSE: Used by the Dan people (of Africa) to connect with the spiritual realm, and as a protective guardian against evil.

LORE: The Dan people use masks in ceremonies or rituals to communicate with spirits and deities. This can be done in hopes of finding protection, guidance, good fortune and more.

ASHANTI MASK

PURPOSE: The Ashanti (Asante) people of Ghana use masks such as this to represent spiritual awareness and protection.

LORE: Often used to honor the dead, bridge into the spiritual realm of gods and deities, as well as bring guidance and power.

Ashanti Mask • Ghana

Harvest Mask • Ghana

HARVEST MASK

PURPOSE: The Dagomba people of Ghana use masks such as this to connect and communicate with gods and deities for positive purposes.

LORE: Masks such as this one are made by skilled artists and often used in dance to promote abundance, and a good harvest.

BALINESE RANGDA MASK

PURPOSE: Rangda is a fearsome demonic queen in Balinese mythology, strongly associated with death and destruction.
LORE: Masks of this type are thought to carry intense spiritual energy. Mishandling them, especially by someone without proper knowledge of the item, is believed to invite malevolent forces and misfortune.

RANGDA MASK • INDONESIA

Noh Mask • Japan

NOH MASK

PURPOSE: Used in traditional Japanese performances to depict characters such as ghosts, demons, gods, and mythical creatures.

LORE: Certain masks are given characteristics and details to represent spiritual beings. Some believe that bringing these entities to life can create power, and attract energy.

THE MENTAL MASK

This story begins with a hand-carved mask from Indonesia, purchased at a flea market. It was intended to be nothing more than a decorative piece, but for Barbara and Sam Jefferson of Newport, Rhode Island, it became the center of a terrifying chapter in their lives. A chapter that would challenge their sanity, their relationship, and their understanding of the world around them.

Sam had first discovered the mask while walking through the aisles of a crowded indoor market. Despite his usual skepticism about anything supernatural, he had found himself inexplicably drawn to the object. He passed by it several times, each time feeling a growing compulsion to take it home. He kept slowly strolling by the item, until finally, he gave in. To Barbara, it was just another purchase. It seemed like a strange but harmless addition to their otherwise serene home. But soon after the mask found its place on their wall, their lives began to change.

It began as minuscule occurrences—flickering lights, an odd chill in the room, and the dogs barking at something unseen. Then the headaches began, as well as strange sounds in the night, and an unsettling sense that they were no longer alone. Barbara, a practical and well grounded woman, began to feel her thoughts slipping away whenever she was near the mask. Her mind, as she described it, felt "hijacked," leaving her unable to think clearly or focus. Sam dismissed these experiences as coincidence or imagination, but his own behavior began to shift in ways Barbara could not ignore. He became distant, cold, and almost protective of the mask. Barbara found him around it constantly, adjusting it often, and even speaking to it as if it were alive.

Their once harmonious home then turned into a battleground. Barbara felt isolated, and trapped in a reality where her fears were dismissed. Sam seemed inexplicably enthralled by an object that Barbara believed was at the center of all their problems. The tension between them grew as the strange occurrences escalated. Shadows appeared in the corners of rooms; voices seemed to murmur from nowhere. The last experience Barbara endured was so unnerving, that it brought her to tears.

Out of desperation for answers and relief, Barbara reached out to us. When we arrived at their home, we were struck by the quiet tension that filled the air. She greeted us warmly, and her relief at our presence was evident. Sam, on the other hand, remained distant, his skepticism palpable. The mask sat in its place on the wall, unassuming yet commanding attention, as if it were aware of our arrival.

The story of this mask is more than just a tale of paranormal phenomena. It is an attestation to the power of belief, the fragility of perception, and the ways in which the unknown can infiltrate even the most grounded of lives. This case is not just about a haunted artifact; it's about the profound impact that the unexplainable can have on relationships, personal truths, and the delicate line between what is real, and what is imagined.

As you read this next case file, we invite you to look beyond the surface, and question what you know about the world around you. Some objects carry stories of their own, but others, like this mask, seem to create them—leaving behind echoes that ripple through the lives they touch. This is Case #051121, The Mental Mask—the story of a family who dared to confront one item's mysteries.

CASE FILE

THE PARANORMAL COUPLE'S
HAUNTED MUSEUM OF

NAME: THE MENTAL MASK

CASE#: 051121

DATE: May 11, 2021

CASE #: 051121 - The Mental Mask

CLIENT NAME: Barbara Jefferson
ALL OCCUPANTS AT LOCATION: Barbara (Client), Husband Sam, 2 Dogs
DATE OF CASE: Winter & Spring of 2021
DATE CLIENT OBTAINED OBJECT: January of 2021
CLIENT LOCATION: Newport, Rhode Island
LOCATION OBTAINED: Indoor Flea Market
OBJECT MANUFACTURE ORIGIN: Handmade - Indonesia

POINT OF CONTACT
EMAIL SENT TO PARANORMAL COUPLE ACCOUNT:
From: *******************@email.com
Date: May 11, 2021 at 6:55:28 PM EST
To: contact@paranormalcouple.com (WEBSITE)
Subject: NONE

Hello my name is Barbara Jefferson and my husband Sam is dealing with some supernatural energies.
In January he bought this old mask and ever since he brought it home it has been driving me up a wall. I can't stand the thing in my house any longer. Neither can our dogs. It's driving us all crazy. Except for him. If you are accepting donations to the museum, please let me know. I would be more than happy to give this to you guys.

Thank you!

PRELIMINARY PHONE INTERVIEW

PHONE INTERVIEW BY: Cody Ray DesBiens & Satori Hawes
DATE: Saturday - May 15, 2021
CLIENT NAME: Barbara Jefferson
PHONE NUMBER: ***-***-****
EMAIL: ********************@email.com

DESCRIPTION OF OBJECT IN QUESTION:
- Hand carved wooden mask.
- Rope fringe around the outer edge.
- Made in Indonesia.

HOW WAS THE OBJECT OBTAINED:
- The client, along with her husband, were walking the isles of an indoor flea market this past January.
- Sam had apparently walked by the mask several times, and felt like something was telling him to buy it.
- He told Barbara that he was going to "buy it no matter what the cost."
- Sam does NOT believe in ghosts, or the supernatural.

WHY DO YOU THINK THE OBJECT IS THE CAUSE OF THE PARANORMAL ACTIVITY:
- The mask apparently gives off a "weird vibe" that can't be explained through words, according to the client.
- When Barbara is sitting near the mask, her thoughts are supposedly "hijacked" by it.
- She claims that she can "never think straight" or "concentrate on anything."
- She says that she has to leave the room often, and after she does, she immediately feels better.
- They also have 2 dogs that constantly bark and stare at the mask.

HOW LONG HAVE YOU BEEN AT THIS LOCATION?:

- Barbara and Sam have lived at their current location for approximately 10 years.
- The residence, to their knowledge, has never had any paranormal activity or strange occurrences before the mask was brought home.

UNEXPLAINED TEMPERATURE CHANGES:

- Barbara states that on one particular evening, she and Sam were watching TV in the living room when a "horrible feeling" fell over the room.
- When this happened, she (and even Sam) instantly felt freezing cold.
- They claim that it felt like the temperature dropped "at least 20 degrees."

UNEXPLAINED ANOMALIES WITH ELECTRICAL DEVICES:

- Barbara states that on a few occasions, they have witnessed the lights in the living room flicker.
- Sam never attributed this to paranormal activity, but Barbara does.

UNEXPLAINED ILLNESS:

- None Reported.

MANIPULATION OF OBJECTS:

- Nothing major was reported.
- Barbara expressed that they have occasionally noticed the mask crooked on the wall in "an unnatural way."
- Again, Sam usually finds an explanation to brush away any claims. His explanations, however, are seen by Barbara (and us) to be "grasping at straws" (very unlikely explanations).

UNEXPLAINED ODORS:

- None Reported.

UNEXPLAINED SOUNDS:

- On multiple occasions, while laying in bed, both the client and Sam have heard what sounds like "the TV falling off the wall," or something extremely heavy "crashing to the floor."
- When they get up to look, everything is perfectly fine. Nothing is out of place.
- Sam has no explanation for this experience.

UNEXPLAINED VOICES:

- Barbara states that she will be sitting in her living room (within proximity of the mask) and hear what sound like someone screaming in her head.
- Sometimes it will cause intense migraines.
- There have also been a few occasions in which Barbara and Sam will be watching TV, and will both hear a man's voice talking in the background.
- She states that it is hard to locate which direction the voice is coming from, but when they mute the TV, it begins to stop.
- Sam thinks that the "room's acoustics might be causing an illusion."
- On another occasion, Barbara was at home alone, and began to hear some sort of "chanting."
- She became emotional while telling this story.
- Barbara states that she feels as though she is being mentally "tortured." She claims that while she was hearing the chanting, she felt like she was going crazy because she couldn't decide if she was actually hearing it with her ears, or if it was in her head.

APPARITIONS/VISUAL ANOMALIES:

- On one occasion last week, Barbara states that she saw a tall, slim figure moving from their bedroom, to the back sliding door.
- This really disturbed her. So much so, in fact, that she didn't even tell Sam about it.
- She claims that he wouldn't have believed her anyway.

PHYSICAL CONTACT:
- On multiple occasions, Sam has supposedly been "poked over and over again, on his shoulders and back."
- The client states that on occasion, the dogs react like something had pulled on their tails, or pushed on their backs.
- She states that the way the dogs react and move is extremely abnormal.

OTHER NOTES:
- Barbara is convinced that her husband is "completely blinded from what is happening."
- It is making her "feel crazy" because she can see him reacting to the same unnerving events, but he always claims that it is something "normal."
- She also believes that Sam may have some sort of "attachment" to the mask.
- Barbara states that she has never seen him be so "caring" for an object.
- He is always "adjusting it," and sometimes "even talks to it."

DESIRED RESULT / OUTCOME:
- Barbara wants the mask GONE.
- She claims that she has convinced Sam to get rid of it.
- They have gotten into multiple arguments over it, and she has told him that "it will only get worse."
- Barbara states that she feels as though she "can not think without the mask listening... and can't stand it any longer."

INVESTIGATOR NOTES:
- Satori and myself have made arrangements to pick up the mask on Friday - May 28, 2021 in Newport, RI.
- Before removal of the mask, we will have to ask Sam directly if he wants the mask gone. We CAN NOT remove the mask if Sam is NOT in agreement.
- If Sam is not in agreement, we will help Barbara with some suggestions to coexist with the mask.

IN-PERSON VISIT TO LOCATION

DATE OF VISIT: Friday - May 28, 2021
INVESTIGATORS PRESENT: Cody Ray DesBiens & Satori Hawes
LOCATION RESIDENTS PRESENT: Barbara (Client), Husband Sam, 2 Dogs

PRELIMINARY NOTES UPON ARRIVAL:

- We were immediately met by the client at the front door. She then introduced us to Sam.
- The home is very nice, and clean.
- There is a finished basement, first floor, second floor, and an attic space.
- Sam did not seem too keen on meeting with us, but seemed emotionally content.
- It is very clear that he is not interested in the paranormal, nor believes in it.

CLOSING NOTES OF IN-PERSON VISIT:

- The mask is now in our possession.
- It was sitting within a bag on the kitchen table.
- Before removing the object from the home, we asked Sam directly if this was something that he wanted, or was okay with being removed.
- He replied with this statement: "Take it away. I'm done with it anyway."
- Barbara was in disbelief by this statement, and told us that she did not know what he meant by that.
- We left the home, and told her that we would be checking in on her in about a week or so (by telephone.)

NOTES:

DATE OF ENTRY TO MUSEUM: Saturday - May 29, 2021

- Today, Satori and I placed the mask within the quarantine room to observe it for the next two weeks.
- We hung the mask in a similar way to how it was at the client's home. We did this in the hopes of backing up the claim that it makes itself "crooked."

CLIENT FOLLOW UP: Sunday - June 13, 2021 - PHONE CALL
- The client stated how grateful she was that we were able to help.
- She states that Sam has "gone back to the way he used to be, before the mask."
- She states that his personality has completely changed back "for the better." Sam then joined the phone call on another line.
- He apologized to us for being "short" with his words during our meeting.
- He realizes that something was "off" with him, and he surprisingly attributes this to the mask.
- We find that this is normal in these circumstances. There have been multiple cases that we have investigated in which individuals do not know that they are being affected, until the paranormal events are over.
- Barbara also mentioned that there have been no other abnormal events with their dogs.

IMPORTANT UPDATE: September & October of 2021
- Over the past few months, we have displayed the mask within our traveling exhibition (at events).
- On multiple occasions, at different locations, unrelated individuals have reported emotional changes occurring when close to the mask.
- A few individuals (who claim to be sensitive to emotions) have directly pointed this mask out as the cause of emotional distress.
- There was one occasion, at an event in Connecticut, in which multiple guests claimed that the mask became crooked on its own. We do not have documented evidence to support this claim, however.

IMPORTANT UPDATE: Saturday - June 17, 2023
- Today, upon entering the museum, we noticed that three masks were on the floor.
- One of those masks was this one.
- One of the other masks was a new addition to the museum. We believe that the energy of this mask may have interfered with the other two.

THE RAM'S REVENGE

The quaint suburban region of Fishers, Indiana, seemed like the perfect backdrop for a quiet and peaceful life. For thirty years, Phil Evans and his wife, Vicki, had made their home there. They truly savored the tranquil charm of their neighborhood. Their home, a modest two-story with a large garden that Vicki tended meticulously, had become a sanctuary filled with memories, comfort, and Phil's unique passion: collecting masks from around the world.

Phil's fascination with masks wasn't just a passing interest—it was a lifelong pursuit. His collection, carefully curated over decades, was a source of pride. Each piece told a story, from the ceremonial masks of Africa, to the ornate designs of Chinese craftsmanship. Displayed along the walls of his study, the masks transformed his room into a gallery of cultural history. For Phil, each mask was a connection to distant lands and traditions, a tangible link to the human experience. But on an unassuming Friday afternoon in May of 2022, that passion took a dark and unexpected turn.

It began as innocently as any other weekend, with Phil and Vicki venturing out on a lunch date. While out, Phil noticed a community garage sale. These sales were usually a treasure hunt for him. It was a chance to unearth hidden gems or overlooked artifacts to add to his personal collection. This was when he spotted it—a mask unlike any he had ever seen before.

The mask was carved from a dark, weathered wood in the likeness of a ram. Its horns curled almost menacingly, and the rough craftsmanship lended it an almost primal allure. Despite its simplicity, the mask seemed to exude a strange energy— a magnetic pull that Phil couldn't quite explain. It wasn't particularly detailed, or presented with any cultural information. Yet, standing there in the driveway of a stranger's home, Phil felt compelled to have it.

The elderly woman selling the mask appeared, almost eager to part with it. Her eyes avoided Phil's as she named a price that was shockingly low. With cash exchanged and the mask in hand, he returned home, unaware of the energy that he had just invited into his life.

At first, the mask seemed like any other addition to his cherished collection. Phil hung it up enthusiastically in his study, alongside all of the others. Its rough edges and ominous design stood out in stark contrast to the vibrant, intricate masks surrounding it. The day then carried on as usual.

But it wasn't long before the atmosphere in their home began to shift. The once-still air grew heavy, charged with an oppressive weight that neither Phil nor Vicki could ignore. The first sign of trouble came late one night when Phil and Vicki were jolted awake by the sound of crashes and bangs. Upon inspection, Phil discovered that multiple objects had fallen without any explanation. Phil's unease grew with each passing day, especially as the disturbances began to center around the new mask.

Then the voices began. Faint, and indistinct, they seemed to echo from afar. No matter how hard Phil and Vicki tried to make out words, the voices seemed to drift just out of range. They were always within proximity of the mask, however.

The item seemed to exert an authority over the house. Motion detectors installed within the house would activate without cause. The lights began flickering on as if responding to an invisible presence. Shadowy figures appeared in the basement windows, fleeting and indistinct, but undeniable.

Despite his rational nature, Phil couldn't ignore the mask's unsettling influence. It became the focal point of his growing fear, its crude face seeming to watch him with a malevolent gaze. For the first time in his decades-long pursuit of collecting masks, Phil felt a connection that he couldn't explain. This feeling was one that grew darker and more oppressive with each passing day.

When he finally reached out for help, the strain in his voice was unmistakable. Phil was not a man prone to superstition or fear, but desperation had left him no other choice. As he recounted the events, his words were tinged with disbelief, as though he himself struggled to accept what had unfolded.

This is Case #051922, The Ram's Revenge—a story of obsession, fear, and a haunted object that tested the boundaries of belief.

CASE FILE

NAME: THE RAM'S REVENGE

CASE#: 051922

DATE: May 19, 2022

CASE #: 051922 - The Ram's Revenge

CLIENT NAME: Phil Evans
ALL OCCUPANTS AT LOCATION: Phil (Client), Wife Vicki
DATE OF CASE: May of 2022
DATE CLIENT OBTAINED OBJECT: Friday - May 13, 2022
CLIENT LOCATION: Fishers, Indiana
LOCATION OBTAINED: Garage Sale
OBJECT MANUFACTURE ORIGIN: Unknown

POINT OF CONTACT
EMAIL SENT TO PARANORMAL COUPLE ACCOUNT:
From: **************@email.com
Date: May 19, 2022 at 11:22:04 PM EST
To: contact@paranormalcouple.com
Subject: HAUNTED OBJECT

Hi
Question. I have a "problematic" mask in my collection and
I do not deal with that type of thing at all. Hoping that you
guys can help with this.
If it's easier to call, my number is ***-***-****
Thanks

Phil

PHONE INTERVIEW BY: Cody Ray DesBiens & Satori Hawes
DATE: Saturday - May 21, 2022
CLIENT NAME: Phil Evans
PHONE NUMBER: ***-***-****
EMAIL: **************@email.com

DESCRIPTION OF OBJECT IN QUESTION:

- Wood mask. Approximately twelve inches long.
- Mask is carved to look like a ram or goat.
- Seems to be a decorative mask due to the fact that it lacks eye holes.

HOW WAS THE OBJECT OBTAINED:

- To begin, the client Phil has an extensive collection of masks from around the world. This has been a hobby of his for decades now.
- As Phil and his wife Vicki were driving to get lunch, they passed by a garage sale. Immediately, the client locked eyes with what looked like a mask. He had to turn around to check it out.
- Once he arrived, he realized that it indeed was a mask. His inner thoughts told him that he "absolutely had to have it, no matter what the cost was."
- He quickly paid the older woman what was owed, hopped back into the car with his wife, and drove off.
- Looking back, the biggest thing he regrets from that day (besides buying the mask) was not asking about its origin, and how the older woman came to own it.

WHY DO YOU THINK THE OBJECT IS THE CAUSE OF THE PARANORMAL ACTIVITY:

- Phil reiterates that he has been collecting masks for years.
- He has never experienced anything like the activity around this mask before, and knows that it is not normal.
- "I find it very ironic that as soon as I bring this thing into my house, my collection hits the floor."
- The client states that he "threw" the mask into the basement after the paranormal events occurred.

HOW LONG HAVE YOU BEEN AT THIS LOCATION?:
- Phil has lived at his current home, with his wife, for about 30 years.
- After the last of their children moved out of their old home, they had purchased their current one.
- It is important to note that the client is the first owner and occupant of this location.

UNEXPLAINED ILLNESS:
- None Reported.

MANIPULATION OF OBJECTS:
- One of the most frightening experiences that Phil and Vicki witnessed happened just days ago.
- In all of his years collecting, nothing like this has ever happened.
- In Phil's display room, he has the masks presented in different ways. Some are in cabinets, some are on tables, and some are hanging on the walls.
- When Phil brought home the newest mask from the garage sale, he did what he usually does after gaining a new piece. He cleaned it off, and then "found the perfect spot for it."
- He hung the mask on one of the walls and claimed that everything looked great.
- Late that night while lying in bed with his wife, they heard a "spine chilling crashing sound." Immediately, Phil had a bad feeling as to what it could be.
- He arose from bed and sprinted to the display room, only to find that most of the masks that were previously on the walls, were now on the floor.
- As he looked around the room in shock, his eyes were once again locked onto the ram mask. It was somehow still hanging on the wall, while every mask around it was on the floor.
- Phil was baffled that all of the hangers were still secured to the wall. It seemed as if the masks would've had to have lifted themselves off of their hooks.
- He is convinced that "whatever is with that ram mask was behind this."

UNEXPLAINED ANOMALIES WITH ELECTRICAL DEVICES:

- Phil states that he has a newer security system that was installed about five years ago.
- Like previously stated, when the big crash occurred, the client "threw" the mask into the basement.
- After doing that, he began to receive alerts that the motion detectors were picking up movement down there. This is still occurring.
- He has gone down to check the space multiple times, and has seen nothing.
- He states that it is not just one sensor doing this, but all three sensors that are down there.
- Phil has expressed that everything was working fine before the mask arrived.

UNEXPLAINED SOUNDS:

- There have been multiple unexplainable sounds that have emanated from the basement.
- It seems that whenever Phil or Vicki opens the basement door, everything stops immediately.
- They both state that there have been sounds of a man and woman talking, a screaming sound, a banging sound, and something that sounds like wood cracking or breaking.
- Once again, the client expressed that none of this was occurring before the new item entered the home.

UNEXPLAINED VOICES:

- Vicki explains that the voices coming from the basement sound like a man and woman having a conversation.
- "It sounds like they are far enough away where you can hear them talking, but you can't make out a word that they are saying."
- Vicki has gone so far as to lay on the floor to see if she can make out any of the words. She states that "it always sounds the same distance away no matter how close I get to it. It's strange!"

UNEXPLAINED TEMPERATURE CHANGES:

- None Reported.

APPARITIONS/VISUAL ANOMALIES:

- Phil states that there has been one occurrence in which he had actually seen something with his own eyes. Two nights ago, both of them went out for the day.
- When they returned, it was now dark outside. Phil remembered that the mail was still sitting in the mailbox.
- Once he retrieved the mail and began walking back toward the house, he saw something very odd.
- "I saw all these shapes moving in the basement windows. It looked like a lava lamp but everything was shades of black. I have never seen anything like that. I immediately ran inside, swung open the basement door, and once again there was nothing."

PHYSICAL CONTACT:

- None Reported.

DESIRED RESULT / OUTCOME:

- Phil wants "peace back in his home."
- He states that collecting masks over the years has been a great source of happiness for him, but now it has been tainted by this experience.
- He simply wants everything to return to the way it was.
- He hopes that the first step in doing that is to get rid of the mask.

INVESTIGATOR NOTES:

- Our first recommendation is to contact the security company to check all sensors. This is to make sure nothing is malfunctioning.
- We also recommended calling a rodent professional. This is to cancel out any idea that the noises could have been made by animals. This of course is a stretch, but we want to make sure all of the boxes are checked.
- Phil also states that they no longer want the mask in the home, so we have instructed them on how to send it to us.

NOTES:

DATE OF ENTRY TO MUSEUM: Friday - May 27, 2022

- Today, Satori and I received the mask in the mail.
- We immediately hung the mask up within the quarantine room for further observation.
- We also hung some empty picture frames around the mask. This is being done to see if anything will move or fall.

IMPORTANT UPDATE: Saturday - May 28, 2022

- Today, we received an email from Phil stating that they are still hearing some noises coming from the basement.
- The security company has already come to the home, and signed off that everything is working properly.
- Phil states that a rodent professional is coming to the house on Monday.
- Just in case it is not rodents, we have suggested that the client state ground rules. We have also recommended that the client state (out loud) that whoever is in his home has to leave now.

IMPORTANT UPDATE: Monday - May 30, 2022

- The client (Phil) has contacted us today to update us that the rodent professional has found no signs of any animal infestation.
- He also stated that they heard a man and woman talking again last night.
- We instructed them to continue to set their ground rules out loud, and sternly.

CLIENT FOLLOW UP: Saturday - June 11, 2022 - PHONE CALL

- Today, Satori and I were able to speak with our client (Phil) and his wife (Vicki) over the phone.
- He states that things have seemingly slowed down a lot. They have only heard a voice once since the last time they checked in with us (about two weeks ago.)
- Overall, they state that things "feel" a lot better in their home.
- We reminded them to continue setting ground rules, even if things seem back to normal.

IMPORTANT UPDATE: Tuesday - June 21, 2022

- Today, Satori and I entered the museum to find two masks on the ground.
- These masks were hanging on either side of the ram mask.
- We suspect that the mask is trying to give us a message. We think that it does not want anything placed around It.
- We hung up the fallen masks in a new spot, and left the area around the ram empty. We hope that this makes the spirit content. Fingers crossed.

EVP: RECORDING SPIRIT SOUNDS AND VOICES

Electronic Voice Phenomena (EVP) refers to mysterious sounds or voices captured on audio recordings. often times, these voices are believed to be communications from spirits or paranormal entities. These sounds are typically not heard while recording, but are discovered during playback. EVPs may manifest as faint whispers, clear words, or unexplained noises.

Here are some tips for conducting a good EVP Session:

Location:
Pick a quiet place with reported activity. Avoid high-traffic areas or places with excessive noise.

Clear Questioning:
Speak slowly, leave 10-20 seconds of silence between questions, and avoid asking multiple things at once.

Minimize Contamination:
Stay still, limit participants, and announce any noises (footsteps, whispering) to avoid false positives.

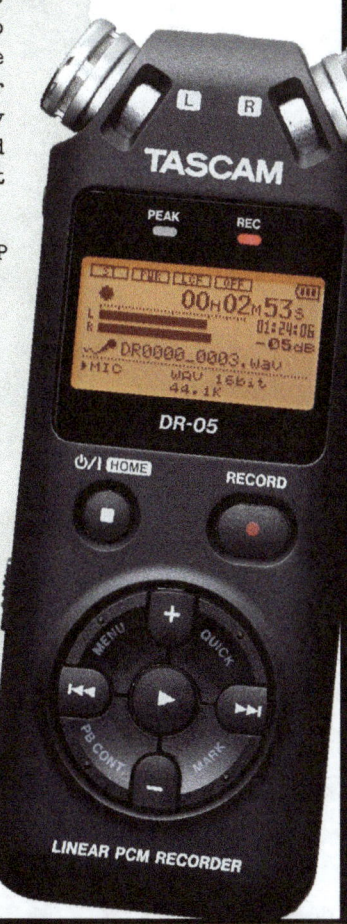

THE ENERGY DRAINER

This case, marked by a chilling transformation within a family's home, began with the arrival of a decorative hand-carved mask in October of 2019. Larry and Deb Peterson of Sanford, Maine, were the items unsuspecting recipients. The mask was a gift from Larry's stepbrother, John, who claimed to have felt an inexplicable compulsion to purchase it after spotting the object in the dusty corner of an antique shop. The mask was seemingly a tourist piece, crafted from sese wood and embellished with metal. The detail of the item bore an eerie elegance. Its round face, hollowed rectangle eyes, and hammered patterns gave the mask a sense of timelessness, as though it carried with it the weight of countless untold stories.

Larry was not known for an interest in tribal or decorative art, making John's choice a curious one. Even so, Larry took an unusual liking to the mask. Deb later recalled how out of character it was for her husband to insist on displaying something so unlike his usual taste. Nevertheless, within hours of unwrapping it, he hung the mask prominently in their living room— directly above the mantelpiece. This is where its presence immediately dominated the space.

Changes within the Peterson household began subtly. The activity was almost undetectable. Within days, Deb found herself inexplicably exhausted— a bone-deep weariness that she couldn't shake, even after a full night's sleep. At first, she attributed this to stress or seasonal fatigue, as October in Maine often brought early chills and shorter days. But soon, the exhaustion began to affect everyone who entered the home. Family members, friends, and even some neighbors who occasionally stepped inside for a chat, remarked on a newly oppressive heaviness in the air.

The house, once a warm and inviting place filled with laughter and chatter, became uncharacteristically silent. The temperature inside the house grew colder, despite the thermostat being set to its usual level. What was most baffling was the sudden and inexplicable spike in their electric bill, suggesting that something within the home was consuming far more energy than usual.

Deb began noticing subtle changes in Larry's demeanor. Once even-tempered and easygoing, he grew irritable and defensive, especially when the mask was brought up. Her casual suggestion to move the mask into a less prominent location sparked an uncharacteristic outburst from Larry, who insisted the mask stay exactly where it was. This reaction left Deb unsettled, as did the way he seemed to spend more time in the living room. He began sitting beneath the mask, distant, in a quiet almost trance-like state.

The turning point came during Thanksgiving, when the Peterson's hosted their extended family for the holiday. Normally a lively occasion filled with warmth, laughter, and the clatter of dishes, this year's gathering was anything but. Relatives commented on the unusual chill of the house, both literal and figurative. Conversations were sluggish, punctuated by long periods of silence. Many attendees also reported feeling inexplicably drained.

The most unsettling incident occurred later that evening. Two relatives fainted inexplicably, their sudden collapses disrupting the tense quiet of the gathering. Both recovered quickly, but were left shaken and unable to explain what had happened. Meanwhile, another family member became transfixed by the mask, sitting silently on the couch for hours, staring up at it with a vacant expression. Attempts to engage her in conversation were met with blank stares, as though she were in a trance.

Later that night, as the house finally emptied and the Peterson's prepared for bed, Larry began hearing a rhythmic drumbeat in his head. It was faint at first, but grew steadily louder and more insistent. The sound was relentless, keeping him awake until dawn. When he finally stumbled downstairs in the early morning light, bleary-eyed and unnerved, he and Deb were met with a chilling sight.

Every small object on the living room tables—candles, coasters, a bowl of keys, and even a pair of reading glasses—had been arranged in a perfect circle directly beneath the mask. Neither Deb nor Larry could explain how, or when, this had occurred. The living room had been undisturbed when they had gone to bed. The arrangement was too precise to be the work of chance, and the sight left them both deeply shaken.

Realizing that they were dealing with something far beyond their understanding, the Peterson's reached out to the museum for help. During our initial interview, Deb spoke of her growing fear for their eleven year old son. While relieved that he hadn't yet shown any effects, she worried that the mask's energy might eventually begin to show itself to him.

Larry's confession during his portion of the interview was equally troubling. Despite the mounting evidence that the mask needed to be removed, he admitted to feeling an inexplicable bond with it, as though a part of him couldn't bear to let it go. He described the sensation as both irrational and irresistible— a pull he couldn't fully explain but knew was unnatural.

This is Case #113019, The Energy Drainer. This case stands out, not only for the mask's powerful influence over the Peterson family, but also for the disturbing sense of compulsion it seemed to exert on anyone who came into contact with it. The events of this case serve as a potent reminder of the unknown powers certain objects may hold, and how effortlessly these powers can enter our lives.

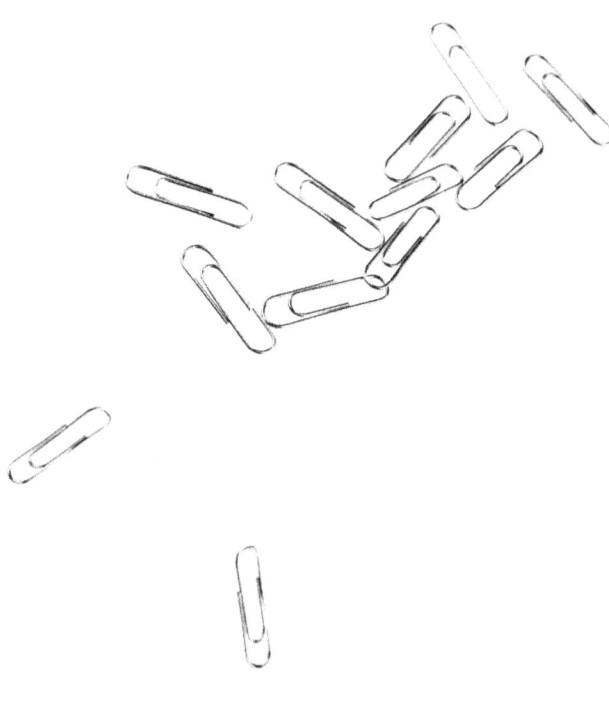

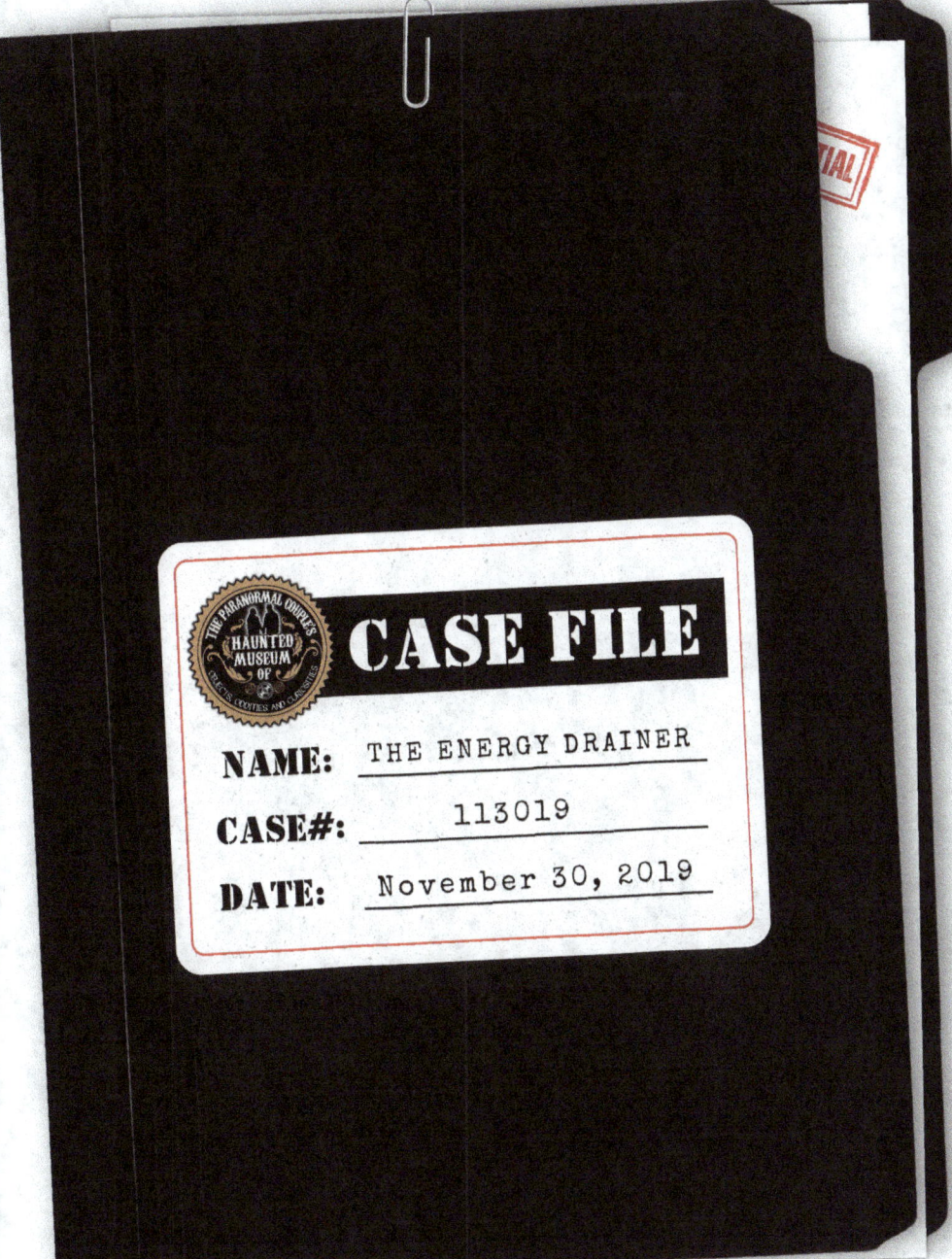

CASE FILE

NAME: THE ENERGY DRAINER

CASE#: 113019

DATE: November 30, 2019

CASE #: 113019 - The Energy Drainer

CLIENT NAME: Deb and Larry Peterson
ALL OCCUPANTS AT LOCATION: Deb (client), Husband Larry, Child John (11)
DATE OF CASE: October & November of 2019
DATE CLIENT OBTAINED OBJECT: October of 2019
CLIENT LOCATION: Sanford, Maine
LOCATION OBTAINED: Random Gift
OBJECT MANUFACTURE ORIGIN: Handmade - African (Ghana)

POINT OF CONTACT
EMAIL SENT TO PARANORMAL COUPLE ACCOUNT:
From: **************@email.com
Date: November 30, 2019 at 11:13:58 PM EST
To: contact@paranormalcouple.com (WEBSITE)
FORM TOPIC: "I Have A Haunted Object"

Hello,
My name is Deb Peterson and my husband's name is Larry. He was given this strange looking mask by his stepbrother and it has drained the energy out of all of us completely. I'm just happy it hasn't affected our son yet. Thanksgiving was a nightmare. We are hoping you can help us. Thank you.

Deb Peterson

EMAIL REPLY SENT FROM PARANORMAL COUPLE ACCOUNT:
To: **************@email.com
Date: December 1, 2019 at 10:30:44 AM EST
From: contact@paranormalcouple.com
RE: "I Have A Haunted Object"

Hello Deb & Larry,

First off, thank you for reaching out to the museum. We are very sorry to hear about the paranormal troubles you are currently facing within your home. Cases of paranormal activity involving children or families become a top priority to us, and we want to do anything we can to help. Let's set up a time to talk on the phone so we can get a better understanding on how to assist you. What day and time is good for you?

- Satori & Cody

PRELIMINARY PHONE INTERVIEW

PHONE INTERVIEW BY: Cody Ray DesBiens & Satori Hawes
DATE: Tuesday - December 3, 2019
CLIENT NAME: Deb Peterson
PHONE NUMBER: ***-***-****
EMAIL: **************@email.com

DESCRIPTION OF OBJECT IN QUESTION:
- Handmade wooden mask. Metal details.
- Seems to be a decorative art piece.

HOW WAS THE OBJECT OBTAINED:
- This past October (2019) Larry's stepbrother randomly visited their home. With him, came the mask.
- He said that he had gotten the mask from an antique store. When the brother first saw it, he stated that he "knew it was meant for him (Larry)."

- This seemed like a very odd and out of place thing for Larry's stepbrother to do.
- To Deb's surprise, her husband "loved" the mask. This was also very strange to her because he does not own anything remotely close to the mask. It isn't something Larry would normally like.
- When the stepbrother left, she asked Larry if he really liked the gift, or if he was just pretending to like it so his step brother was happy. Larry angrily snapped back at her stating that he loves it, and that he is going to hang it in the living room of "his house." This comment made her upset, but she let him hang it up anyway.

WHY DO YOU THINK THE OBJECT IS THE CAUSE OF THE PARANORMAL ACTIVITY:
- Deb states that the entire energy of the house changed as soon as the mask came into the home.
- She noticed that overtime, her energy was also draining. She says that "everything began to feel like it was in slow motion."
- She states that Larry's attitude changed, and everyone who came over to the house became "ill and drained for no reason."

HOW LONG HAVE YOU BEEN AT THIS LOCATION?:
- Deb and Larry moved into this home just before their son John was born (about 12 years ago.)
- The home was originally built by Larry's grandfather in the 1950's. When his grandparents moved into an assisted living home in 2007, Larry purchased the house from them.
- Larry's grandparents never reported anything strange in the home.
- Growing up, he states that neither himself, nor any of his cousins had ever experienced anything paranormal.
- It is also important to state that Larry's grandparents are still alive.

UNEXPLAINED TEMPERATURE CHANGES:
- Deb states that the house seems to be colder since the mask came into the picture.
- She states that their electric bill is "higher than usual for this time of year because the heat keeps kicking on more than usual."

UNEXPLAINED ANOMALIES WITH ELECTRICAL DEVICES:
- None Reported.

UNEXPLAINED ILLNESS:
- Besides Deb feeling drained constantly, the biggest event happened on Thanksgiving.
- Every year, the Peterson's hold Thanksgiving at their home to continue the family tradition that Larry's grandparents started.
- Usually, every Thanksgiving is wonderful, but this year "was very different."
- Deb states that they had about 10 people over their house, and that every one of them felt "different."
- "Most of them felt like they had run a marathon and needed to sleep." She also stated that 2 people passed out for no reason at all.
- One family member was acting "odd" and sat in front of the mask all day long, staring at it. Deb expressed that whenever someone would try to have a conversation with the person, they would respond with short answers to end the conversation.

MANIPULATION OF OBJECTS:
- The mask hangs on a nail where a picture used to be. Deb has found the mask "crooked" multiple times.
- One of the creepiest events happened the morning after Thanksgiving.
- She states that when they woke up, they had found every small object that was previously on top of their coffee and end tables moved. Now they were sitting in a circle in the center of the living room floor, directly under the mask.
- This was extremely strange, and freaked the family out.

UNEXPLAINED ODORS:
- None Reported.

UNEXPLAINED VOICES:
- None Reported.

UNEXPLAINED SOUNDS:

- Thanksgiving night, after the extended family members left, Larry began to hear a "drumming beat" in his head.
- He repeatedly asked his wife if she had heard it too, but she never did.
- He was up for most of the night, but eventually went to sleep. When he woke up the next morning, it was gone.
- That morning was the same morning that they had found the ring of objects on the floor.

APPARITIONS/VISUAL ANOMALIES:

- Deb states that she sometimes "sees shadows out of the corner of her eye," but she is not fully convinced that it is 100% paranormal.

PHYSICAL CONTACT:

- None Reported.

OTHER NOTES:

- After Thanksgiving, and the drumming, Larry is now aware that the mask seems to be the cause of people feeling drained. He now sees that he may have an attachment to it.
- He states that "it feels like something inside of me is telling me that I need to keep the mask, but my brain is telling me that it has to go for my family's sake."

DESIRED RESULT / OUTCOME:

- Deb and Larry are both in agreement that the object needs to leave the house.
- They are hoping that once the mask is gone, everyone will feel back to normal again.

INVESTIGATOR NOTES:

- Satori and I (Cody) think that it would be important to speak with Larry's stepbrother to ask why he randomly gifted the mask.
- He has agreed to speak with us over the phone on 12/5/19.
- We have also instructed the client on where to send the mask.

PHONE INTERVIEW BY: Cody Ray DesBiens & Satori Hawes
DATE: Thursday - December 5, 2019
CLIENT NAME: Brian Peterson
PHONE NUMBER: ***-***-****

WHERE DID THE MASK COME FROM:

- Larry's stepbrother (Brian) states that the mask was purchased at an antique store.
- He claims that as soon as he locked eyes with the mask, he heard his stepbrother's name in his head. He knew that he had to buy it for him.

DID YOU FEEL DIFFERENT AFTER GIFTING THE MASK:

- "I felt like my job was done. I didn't care what he did with it after I gave it to him. I felt like my only job was to get it to him, and that's it. I felt accomplished."

HAVE YOU FELT TIRED OR DRAINED SINCE YOU FOUND THE MASK:

- Brian states that the only time he has felt tired is when he went over Deb and Larry's home for Thanksgiving.

CLOSING NOTES OF SECOND PHONE INTERVIEW:

- This is the first time that we have observed another individual feeling a "magnetic pull" to purchase an object for someone else.
- It seems like Brian was only used as a stepping stone to get the mask to the client (Larry.)
- We do not believe that the stepbrother was trying to intentionally harm or distress the client in any way.

NOTES:

DATE OF ENTRY TO MUSEUM: Wednesday - December 11, 2019

- Today, we received the mask, and placed it within the quarantine room. We plan to observe it for the next two or three weeks.
- We will now begin research on the object's origin.

IMPORTANT UPDATE: Sunday - December 15, 2019

- Over the past few weeks we have been researching the mask to see if we can find its maker, and meaning.
- After an extensive search, we have found that the mask is indeed an art piece from Ghana, in West Africa.
- The mask was carved by hand from sese wood with aluminum accents. It was most likely sold at either a market, or online. It must have found its way to an antique store sometime after that.
- The artist is still alive. We believe that the mask design is titled Kafui, which means 'praise him' in the Ewe language.
- The design is described by the artist as a "person with a round face singing praises to God." Multiple variations of this mask exist.
- What remains unknown to us is who brought the mask to the United States, and what happened to the mask before it ended up in the stepbrother's hands? Those are two questions we will never have answers to.

CLIENT FOLLOW UP: Friday - December 20, 2019 - PHONE CALL

- We were able to reach our client over the phone.
- Deb stated that Larry's attitude seems to be back to normal, and that the house's energy also seems "great again."
- She states that the extended family has returned to the home with "no new incidents."
- She is very grateful that the mask is gone, and she hopes to never see it again.

IMPORTANT UPDATE: Saturday - September 24, 2022

- Today, we had the mask on display at a local event.
- One person at the event (without knowing the backstory of this item) began to stare at the mask for an unusual amount of time.
- After a few minutes, I (Cody) approached the woman to stop her from zoning out.
- We feel like something may have been drawing her into the mask.

HANDCRAFTED HAUNTS:

HANDMADE ITEMS THAT BECAME HAUNTED

HANDMADE THINGS

✳ Emotional Imprint: A creator's intense emotions—joy, sorrow, anger—may transfer to their work during the crafting process.

✳ Unfinished Business: The creator passed away or abandoned the project before completing it, possibly leaving unresolved energy tied to the object.

✳ Legacy of Creation: Passed down through generations, the object may carry the compounded energies and memories of its previous makers and owners.

There's something deeply personal about handmade objects. Each stitch, chisel mark, or brushstroke carries a piece of the creator's spirit— a reflection of their passion, pain, or purpose. But sometimes, this connection can run far deeper than intended, tethering the object to its maker in ways that defy explanation. When human emotion, intention, or tragic circumstances become woven into the fabric of creation, the result can be more than just art. Creation can become a vessel for the supernatural.

Some of the most intriguing, and unsettling pieces within our museum are unfinished works. They are remnants of people's lives left by sudden illness, or unexpected tragedy. It seems that with some objects, the original owners never seemed to let go— even after passing on.

Some researchers believe that a powerful attachment to an unfinished project can create a psychic bond. An artist who dedicated years to a masterpiece, a writer whose story lay half-written, a carpenter halfway through building a piece of furniture— each of these artists poured time, emotion, and intention into their craft. When people pass away before their work is complete, it's believed that part of their spirit may linger, unable or unwilling to abandon a task that was, to them, deeply meaningful.

In other cases, the object itself may hold a kind of "memory." A recording of time charged with the energy and intention of its maker. Paranormal researchers call this a "Residual Haunting." In relation to haunted objects, this form of activity occurs when the object simply holds onto the emotion and interaction that was poured into it, or exposed to it, during the creation process.

There's a reason people say, "You can feel the love in this work." Artists, craftsmen, and builders pour their emotion into their works, channeling their energy into something tangible. The items are imbued with intent, energy, and sometimes, fragments of the soul. This, in turn, creates something not only tangible, but paranormal. But when life interrupts or ends, especially if a piece is left unfinished, a strange, lingering presence can be imprinted on the object itself. It's as if the creator's hands still yearn to complete the task, even from beyond the grave.

Some paranormal investigators, researchers, and theorists believe that it's not just memory and energy stamped onto these types of objects, however. Many believe that it's the soul of a person, unable or unwilling to let go— haunted by their own need to watch over their creation.

Handmade haunted objects are unique because they hold more than a form and function. They hold fragments of life, as well as fragments of time. Whether the result of an unfinished dream, a passion, or the intent to affect others in some way or form, these objects blur the line between art and the metaphysical. They remind us that what we make with our hands can carry more than we originally intended. They can sometimes bridge into realms we cannot see.

The stories that follow delve into the origins of specific objects, and the ties that bind them to their creators. Each case serves as evidence to the power of human connection, creativity, and the mysteries that arise when material and metaphysical begin to cross. As you explore these accounts, consider this: What we make with our hands may outlast us, but at what cost, and to what end?

THE GHOST SHIP

The autumn air was heavy with loss and memory— pressing gently upon a quiet suburban home in Hartford, Connecticut. Inside lies the workshop of Edward Bennet, a retired gentleman who loved to build intricate model ships from scratch. Edward had begun to build a beautiful yet elaborate model, a large four-masted ship. He carefully carved each plank, and shaped each sail with incredible precision. His health, however, began to decline rapidly due to a terminal illness. Edward unfortunately passed away before the ship could be completed.

While Edward's family mourned his loss, they noticed strange occurrences within his workshop. Once a space of creativity and peacefulness, the workshop began to come alive in ways no one could explain. Objects would shift and tools would clatter, as if unseen hands were restlessly moving them. Lights flickered with uncanny timing, coldness would descend without warning, and family would catch the faint but unmistakable scent of cigar smoke on more than one occasion. Edwards' daughter Madison began to hear faint sounds of wood scraping, hammering, and even whispered curses. Edward's presence seemed to ripple throughout the space that he had left behind.

The family clung to the notion that these strange occurrences were not a threat, but rather a sign. It seemed to be a loved one's attempt to finish what he had started. But as time wore on, the uneasy feeling grew stronger, and the once-beloved workshop became a place to avoid. Each member of the household felt an odd compulsion to respect the ghostly claim that seemed to have staked over the ship. Edward's widow Dawn, though touched by the signs of her husband's spirit, felt herself growing wearier with each incident. Her grief was compounded by an unsettling feeling that he may not be at rest.

And so, the call for help was sent out to us. It came to us with a request as delicate as the ship itself: to bring closure, to bring calm, and to find a place where the vessel and lingering spirit might finally be settled to rest. It was more than a request for assistance; it was a heartfelt plea from a family seeking to honor the past, while also freeing themselves from its lingering shadows. This was not just about a haunting; it was about a family yearning to reclaim their lives from the restless grasp of a love left incomplete.

Edward's family ultimately decided to donate the ship to the museum. For us, this was not just a matter of taking in another artifact; it was a profound responsibility. Like all other objects, we placed the ship within The Quarantine Room. After its inclusion within the museum, subtle yet undeniable phenomena would unfold around the ship. On one occasion, we discovered tiny wood shavings scattered around the model, with no visible explanation. It was as if Edward had never left his workshop, his spirit still tirelessly devoted to his beloved project.

The activity was never aggressive or alarming, but rather, it carried a quiet persistence—a sense of determination and care. When we finally moved the model into our general exhibition area, The Ghost Ship, as it came to be known, continued to reveal its unmistakable energy. Visitors to our exhibits often stopped to remark on the strange, yet comforting atmosphere surrounding the model. Some described a gentle breeze brushing past them as they stood near it, while others reported a sensation of being watched. There was never a sense of malice, but rather, a deep and abiding affection.

This case also raised intriguing questions about the nature of hauntings. Was Edward's spirit truly tied to the model, or was it the powerful emotional resonance of his final project that lingered? Could his unyielding love for his craft have imprinted itself so deeply on the object that it took on a life of its own? If so, what does that say about the objects we cherish in life, and the ways they might carry traces of us after we're gone?

This is Case #100219, The Ghost Ship—the story of a passion so profound, that even a final breath could not extinguish the desire to see a project finished. To this day, Edward's ship sits quietly within its display, sometimes swaying ever so slightly. Its presence reminds us that some journeys, even in death, are never truly over.

CASE FILE

NAME: THE GHOST SHIP

CASE#: 100219

DATE: October 2, 2019

CASE #: 100219 - "The Ghost Ship"

CLIENT NAME: Dawn Bennet
ALL OCCUPANTS AT LOCATION: Widow Dawn (Sometimes daughter Madison, son Jake, & grandchildren)
DATE OF CASE: October 2020
DATE CLIENT OBTAINED OBJECT: September of 2020
CLIENT LOCATION: Hartford, CT
LOCATION OBTAINED: Handmade by late husband
OBJECT MANUFACTURE ORIGIN: Not Applicable

POINT OF CONTACT
EMAIL SENT TO PARANORMAL COUPLE ACCOUNT:
From: *********@email.com
Date: October 2, 2020 at 6:02:43 PM EST
To: contact@paranormalcouple.com
Subject: My husband's ship

Hey Paranormal Couple,
This is Dawn Bennet. I was wondering if you could lend me some paranormal assistance if you have some spare time. I know you both are very busy, but I am a little freaked out and would truly appreciate it if you could give me a call.

Thank you kindly,

Dawn
Cell Phone: ***-***-****

PRELIMINARY PHONE INTERVIEW

PHONE INTERVIEW BY: Cody Ray DesBiens
DATE: October 6, 2020
CLIENT NAME: Dawn Bennet
PHONE NUMBER: ***-***-****
EMAIL: *********@email.com

DESCRIPTION OF OBJECT IN QUESTION:
- Handcrafted model ship.
- Approximately 1.5 feet in length, and 2 feet in height.

HOW WAS THE OBJECT OBTAINED:
- The client's (Dawn) recently deceased husband (Edward) built detailed model ships as a hobby.
- This ship was the last project that he was working on before passing.

WHY DO YOU THINK THE OBJECT IS THE CAUSE OF THE PARANORMAL ACTIVITY:
- Building ship's was Ed's passion.
- Soon after passing away, paranormal activity started in the home.
- The client states that she and her family "knew it was him right away."
- All activity seems to be happening within vicinity of the ship.

HOW LONG HAVE YOU BEEN AT THIS LOCATION?:
- Dawn has lived at this location with her husband for the past 45 years.
- They have 2 grown adult children together (Madison and Jake) who no longer live on the property. They visit a few times a week with their children.

UNEXPLAINED TEMPERATURE CHANGES:
- "Extreme cold spots" in Ed's workshop.
- On one occasion, Dawn and her family experienced what they describe as a "cold wall" that stopped them in their tracks.

UNEXPLAINED ANOMALIES WITH ELECTRICAL DEVICES:

- The lights in the home seem to flicker on command. This has happened on a few occasions.
- The client will oftentimes find Ed's workshop light turned on with no explanation.

UNEXPLAINED ILLNESS:

- None Reported.

MANIPULATION OF OBJECTS:

- Soon after Ed passed away, objects within his work area "seemed to come alive."
- The closet door in the hallway seems to open by itself.
- Dawn states that her husband used to keep his hat and coat in this closet.
- She also mentioned that his clothing is still untouched. His garments are in the same area that he left them before passing.

UNEXPLAINED ODORS:

- Cigar Smoke has been smelled at two family gatherings by multiple people.

UNEXPLAINED SOUNDS:

- Dawn and her family have all heard what sounds like tools moving in Ed's workshop.
- Footsteps, and loud crashing sounds have also occurred throughout the home. The sounds can't be explained.
- On one occasion, Dawn states that it sounded like her husband's radio turned on by itself in the workshop.
- When the client went to check on the radio, she found that it was powered "off," and unplugged from the wall.

UNEXPLAINED VOICES:

- Dawn states that on her birthday, she clearly heard what sounded like Ed yelling her name.
- This both comforted her, and saddened her at the same time.

APPARITIONS/VISUAL ANOMALIES:
- None Reported.

PHYSICAL CONTACT:
- None Reported.

OTHER NOTES:
- Dawn and her family feel 100% certain that the paranormal activity is being caused by Ed.
- She made it clear that there was no paranormal activity before his passing.
- Mostly all activity revolves around Ed's workshop, and model ship.

DESIRED RESULT / OUTCOME:
- Even though Dawn and her family are certain that it is Ed causing most of the activity, they are still very creeped out by all of the activity.
- They feel that because this ship was the last project he was working on, there is "unfinished business." The client feels like Edward still wants to finish building it.
- Dawn wants to donate the ship to the museum.

INVESTIGATOR NOTES:
- Satori and myself have requested that Dawn move the ship into a shed that is on her property.
- We are hoping to see a change in activity within the home.
- We will be making an in person visit to the location on 10/17/20.

VISIT TO LOCATION

DATE OF VISIT: Saturday - October 17, 2020
INVESTIGATORS PRESENT: Cody Ray DesBiens & Satori Hawes
LOCATION RESIDENTS PRESENT: Client (Dawn) & her daughter Madison

PRELIMINARY NOTES UPON ENTRY:

- Dawn, and her daughter Madison, gave us a tour of the home. There is a finished basement, first floor, second floor, and a small attic space.
- Home seems very clean and organized.

PARTIAL AUDIO TRANSCRIPT:

(The following audio was recorded at the kitchen table located on the first floor of the client's home. Date is 10/17/20 at 6:32pm ET. Satori, myself, the client Dawn, & her daughter Madison were present. This is a partial transcription.)

CODY: Just to start, I know this may be a touchy subject, but can you tell us a bit about your husband?

DAWN: Sure! No problem at all. He was one of those guys that would've given the shirt off his back to help someone out. Just a really really nice man who left us way too early.

MADISON: He was incredible, we all miss him.

SATORI: How long did Ed build the ships for?

DAWN: I believe his entire life, pretty much. I know for as long as I've known him, he was always working on some sort of model. He really got into the ships about 20 years ago. He started with the small ships in the bottles, and gradually got an interest in building larger models.

CODY: Wow! That is awesome. Definitely takes patience to do those tiny ships in a bottle.

DAWN: He loved doing it, and he was great at it!

CODY: He sure was!

SATORI: He definitely is.

CODY: So just to recap, why do you think the activity is revolving around Ed's ship?

CLIENT: Well, we had no ghosts in this house before he died. After he passed, it seems like the house kind of came alive. No matter where we move the ship, it seems like the ghost will follow it.

CODY: Wow. Interesting...

SATORI: What is the first thing that you remember happening?

MADISON: Well, I know that the first thing that I remember happening was hearing the loud footsteps in the workshop one day.

DAWN: And the first thing I can recall was seeing some of his tools moving around on his work bench.

CODY: Did you see them moving? Or just notice that things weren't in their right spots?

DAWN: I actually saw them moving on their own... It really freaked me out.

CODY: What the heck! Did you notice a difference in activity after you moved the ship to the shed?

DAWN: Yes! It was very clear that everything going on, ghost wise, is attached to the ship because it all went away when we put it out there.

SATORI: Interesting... I'm sure he is probably checking in on it, and wants to finish it.

DAWN: I agree. But it's just freaky to me. We know it's Ed, but we want him to rest. We know he will watch over us no matter if the ship is here or not. Now I'm afraid to go into the shed alone. I just would like you both to take it if possible. It would make me feel a lot better.

DAWN: I think it would also be a nice tribute to show off Ed's work to the people that come to visit your museum. I think they will love all of the little details.

CODY: We can absolutely do that if you'd like, but please remember that if you ever want it back at some point, just contact us and we will get it back to you ASAP.

(The rest of the conversation was rather brief. It seems like the family wants the ship to be removed.)

CLOSING NOTES OF IN PERSON VISIT:
- Satori and myself have removed the ship from the client's shed, and into the back of our museum truck.
- Dawn's emotional state already seems a bit better now that the ship is in our possession.
- We will be checking in with the family, by phone, in about two weeks.

NOTES:
CLIENT FOLLOW UP: Friday - November 6, 2020 - PHONE CALL
- We were able to reach our client over the telephone.
- Dawn states that all paranormal activity inside the home has stopped. She is very grateful to not be "freaked out" anymore.

IMPORTANT UPDATE: Tuesday - July 19, 2022
- Today, while dusting the museum, we noticed something strange near the ship.
- On the shelf, around the front of the item, we found small wood shavings. The shavings appear similar to what a piece of sandpaper would cause.
- We have no normal explanation for the shavings.
- There is no damage to the shelf. There is no sign of insects, rodents, or anything that may cause wood damage within the museum.
- Satori and I have cleaned the shelf so it will be easy to spot if it happens again.

THE KNEELING STATUE

In the quiet shadow of summer, Wallingford Connecticut seemed an unlikely setting for a tale of the paranormal. Life in this small town moved at its usual pace, with its familiar streets and modest homes offering a sense of steady normalcy. But for Robert Price, a retired craftsman grappling with the weight of illness, life had shifted into something far more profound, and deeply personal. As the world around him stood still, his own days were marked by a mix of both uncertainty and reflection.

Robert's world had narrowed down to the walls of his home, the gentle presence of his wife, Rita, and the constant solace he sought through prayer and devotion. Faced with the inevitability of life's closing chapter, he sought refuge in his craft. It was a skill he had honed over the years, and one that now became a lifeline for his emotions. Each wood carving he created was a prayer in itself, a silent testament to his faith and resilience.

Among his many creations, one stood apart. It was not merely another piece of firewood transformed into art, but a seven-inch wooden statue of profound religious significance. To an untrained eye, it might have seemed just like any other devotional object. Its smooth lines and intricate details are the mark of a practiced hand. Yet, for Robert, this carving was more than an expression of faith. It was an extension of his spirit, a symbol of his journey, and, as he would soon discover, a connection to something far beyond the natural world.

The moment that would alter the course of his final days came on an otherwise unremarkable evening. Kneeling in prayer before the statue, Robert claimed to witness the extraordinary. He said the figure moved, its wooden face seeming to shift with life. A voice, gentle but clear, then began to speak to him. The message was simple yet profound: it was reassurance and comfort in the face of his fears. The voice told him that his pain would soon fade, and that peace awaited him.

From that night forward, everything changed. The fear and anguish that had weighed so heavily on Robert lifted, replaced by a sense of calm and acceptance. The statue, once a simple carving, became a beacon of hope.

It became an anchor in his final journey. Robert's days, though numbered, were no longer clouded by despair.

Yet this story is far from a straightforward tale of solace. The statue began to reveal mysteries that unsettled even the most accepting of minds. On occasion, the air around it would fill with a soft, untraceable scent of flowers. On other occasions, an inexplicable warmth seemed to radiate from the figure, enveloping those near it in a sensation of peace and healing. Though it never moved again, the faint echo of a voice was sometimes heard during prayer, as if the carving still carried whispers from beyond.

This is Case #060920, The Kneeling Statue. It is a story that blurs the line between the seen and unseen, as well as the line between faith and the supernatural. Was the statue merely a reflection of Robert's unwavering belief? Acting as a comforting projection of his own inner strength? Or was it, as some might wonder, a vessel for something far greater; something not bound by the physical world? Whatever the answer, the story of the kneeling statue continues to inspire, challenge, and comfort all who encounter it.

CASE FILE

NAME: THE KNEELING STATUE

CASE#: 060920

DATE: June 9, 2020

CLIENT NAME: Robert Price
ALL OCCUPANTS AT LOCATION: Robert (Client), (Wife) Rita, Pet Cat
DATE OF CASE: June 2020
DATE CLIENT OBTAINED OBJECT: Handmade in 2019
CLIENT LOCATION: Wallingford, Connecticut
LOCATION OBTAINED: Handmade by client in home
OBJECT MANUFACTURE ORIGIN: Handmade

POINT OF CONTACT
EMAIL SENT TO PARANORMAL COUPLE ACCOUNT:
From: ***********@email.com
Date: June, 9 2020 at 3:12:52 PM EST
To: contact@paranormalcouple.com (WEBSITE)
Subject: My Story

Dear Satori and Cody,

My name is Robert and I have a story to tell that is too long for me to type. If you wouldn't mind calling me on the telephone it would be much appreciated.
Thank you.

--****

Kind Regards,

Rob

PRELIMINARY PHONE INTERVIEW

PHONE INTERVIEW BY: Cody Ray DesBiens & Satori Hawes
DATE: Friday - June 11, 2020
CLIENT NAME: Robert Price
PHONE NUMBER: ***-***-****
EMAIL: ***********@email.com

DESCRIPTION OF OBJECT IN QUESTION:
- Hand carved religious statue (Roman Catholic).
- Made of wood.
- Approximately 7 inches tall.

HOW WAS THE OBJECT OBTAINED:
- The client (Rob) has been terminally ill for the past 2 years.
- After he retired from his full time job, he wanted to try something new to pass the time
- He found an old piece of firewood and decided to try and carve it.
- Rob was hooked, and has been carving wood for the past ten years.
- This item in particular was carved last year (2019) due to Rob's current health situation.
- Unfortunately, Rob was told that he had six months to a year left to live before his illness would eventually take his life.
- During this time, Rob became much closer to his religion (Catholicism) and started to attend church three to five times a week.
- Unfortunately, a few months later, Rob became too ill to travel to church, and was forced to stop attending.
- After this decision was made, Rob's wife (Rita) tried her best to fulfill her husband's wishes, and make him feel comfortable.
- She ended up purchasing a "kneeler" (a piece of furniture used to kneel on during prayer).
- Rob would use this kneeler every morning and evening for prayer.
- He also started carving religious figures that he could pray to.
- The first figure that he carved was this statue.
- When the carving was finished, he attached it to the top of his kneeler, and began praying to it everyday.

WHY DO YOU THINK THE OBJECT IS THE CAUSE OF THE PARANORMAL ACTIVITY:

- One evening, while Rob was finishing his prayers, he was looking at this statue when he claims that it began moving and speaking to him.
- While getting emotional, he stated that the statue told him "You have nothing to worry about. Your pain will soon fade away, and you will be at peace."
- Rob was initially scared to pass away after getting the news that he didn't have much time left to live.
- After this experience, he was completely at peace with his situation.

HOW LONG HAVE YOU BEEN AT THIS LOCATION?:

- Rob and Rita have lived in their home for about 38 years.
- The home has never had any paranormal activity, or unexplainable events.

UNEXPLAINED TEMPERATURE CHANGES:

- Rob states that when the statue spoke to him, an "overwhelming feeling of warmth" fell over him.
- He stated that this feeling made him emotional.

UNEXPLAINED ANOMALIES WITH ELECTRICAL DEVICES:

- None Reported.

UNEXPLAINED ILLNESS:

- The opposite was reported by the client.
- He stated that after this event was over, a lot of his pain went away. He claims that he physically felt a lot better than usual.
- Client reiterates feeling a sense of "warmth."

MANIPULATION OF OBJECTS:

- None Reported.

UNEXPLAINED ODORS:

- An unexplainable floral scent has been experienced on only a few occasions.

UNEXPLAINED SOUNDS:

- None Reported.

UNEXPLAINED VOICES:

- Rob states that he often hears the same voice that he had experienced previously from the statue.
- He hasn't seen the statue move again, but will hear words of encouragement while he prays.

APPARITIONS/VISUAL ANOMALIES:

- None Reported.

PHYSICAL CONTACT:

- None Reported.

DESIRED RESULT / OUTCOME:

- Rob wants to donate his carving to the museum because he believes it to be a symbol of hope for others in their own beliefs.
- He hopes that if an individual crosses paths with the statue, maybe they will receive a message of hope if needed.

INVESTIGATOR NOTES:

- I (Cody) find this story to be compelling due to the fact that Rob's experience is similar to an object that has been passed down in my family for generations.
- The object is a large painting of Christ, and the story that was told to me (Cody) was that my great-grandfather would pray to this painting every night before bed. In the final days of his life, he was also fearful of passing away. This changed, however, after the painting supposedly spoke to him. The painting seemed to come to life, and told him that everything would be okay.

OTHER NOTES:
- Rob has requested to mail the statue due to the current COVID - 19 pandemic. He is at high risk for health complications.
- We will be sure to check in with Rob in a few weeks to see if there have been any paranormal changes, or new events.

NOTES:

DATE OF ENTRY TO MUSEUM: Tuesday - June 23, 2020
- Today, we received the statue in the mail from the client.
- The object will be placed within the quarantine room for about two weeks. Then it will be moved into the religious artifact section of the museum.

CLIENT FOLLOW UP: Saturday - July 25, 2020 - PHONE CALL
- Today, we attempted to make contact with our client (Rob.)
- We spoke to Rita (his wife) who informed us that Rob had sadly passed away, peacefully, a week ago at their home.
- We asked her if she would like us to send the statue back, but she declined.
- She stated that "the carving is where it is supposed to be according to Rob," and "that makes me happy."

IMPORTANT UPDATE: November of 2021
- Over the past year, the statue has been brought to multiple events where individuals have reported feeling a "strong, yet positive energy" coming from the object.
- We will continue to monitor reports from the public.

IMPORTANT UPDATE: October of 2022
- Over the past few months, the "kneeling statue" has been a part of our traveling exhibit.
- Once again, multiple unrelated people have reported an energy radiating from the object.
- Most individuals stated that it was a "warm and positive/happy feeling."

THE WITCH WHISTLE

$\mathbf{F}$or Genevieve Dupont, the stories of her great-grandmother were like fragments of a fading legend, carried down through her family like an heirloom. A practicing witch in early 20th century France, her great-grandmother was said to belong to a coven that casts spells. These spells were used not to curse or harm, but rather, to heal, protect, and promote positive change; particularly in times of hardship. These stories were part of Genevieve's heritage, but they had always seemed distant; more like legend rather than truth.

That changed in 2020.

The Coronavirus pandemic swept through the world like a storm, destroying millions of lives and forcing many to reflect on the past. For Genevieve's mother, it brought to mind one particular story about her grandmother: during an outbreak of an avian-related disease in the early 1900s, the witches in Genevieve's great-grandmother's circle had created spiritual whistles. Fashioned from bone and bird legs, these specific whistles were used as part of a ritual to ward off sickness and destruction. Though Genevieve's mother had never seen one for herself, she remembered the tale vividly. It was a mixture of mystery and folklore, rooted in their family's own history.

Months later, while sifting through the belongings left in her own mother's attic, Genevieve's mother uncovered something extraordinary. There, buried beneath decades of forgotten keepsakes, was one of the actual whistles.

The object itself was larger than an average whistle, delicate, and a bit unsettling in appearance. It was truly a preserved relic from another time. To Genevieve, it felt like a tangible connection to the stories that her mother had grown up hearing. Curious and eager to experience its history, she replaced the old crumbling mouthpiece and, without hesitation, blew into it.

That moment would change everything.

The sound was sharp and haunting. It wasn't just a noise that echoed throughout the room, but also a sensation. It was a feeling that seemed to settle into the very air around them. Both Genevieve and her mother were struck by an overwhelming chill; a creeping discomfort that lingered long after the sound had faded. Others who have heard the whistle reported strange effects: unease, nausea, and an inexplicable sense of angst.

The whistle, Genevieve realized, wasn't just an interesting historic heirloom. It was a vessel, infused with the intention of its creator, carrying echoes of the ritual it had once been a part of. Designed for a single person, with a single purpose, its energies seem misaligned when touched by others.

Recognizing the whistle's potential to harm or unsettle others, Genevieve and her mother made the difficult decision to part with it. She reached out to us with a heartfelt letter, sharing her family's story and offering the artifact to a new home. This way, a piece of history and culture had a place where it could be preserved, studied, and protected. Their hope was that the whistle's history could be honored, and shared with others, without endangering those who encounter it.

When the package arrived, its presence was undeniable. It isn't just an everyday object; it is a thread tied to an extraordinary past. It carries with it the echoes of a powerful practice, and the mysterious life of a woman who had put magic into history.

This is Case #021523, the story of The Witch Whistle. It is a tale of legacy, curiosity, and the unexplainable powers that can linger in objects crafted with purpose. It's a glimpse into a world where history, folklore, and the supernatural intertwine. Let this story serve as a reminder that even the most unique artifacts can carry the weight of the past.

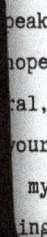

peak
hope
ral,
our
my
ing

CASE FILE

NAME: THE WITCH WHISTLE

CASE#: 021523

DATE: February 2, 2023

THE PARANORMAL COMPLEX
HAUNTED MUSEUM OF
OBJECTS, STATUES, AND CURIOSITIES

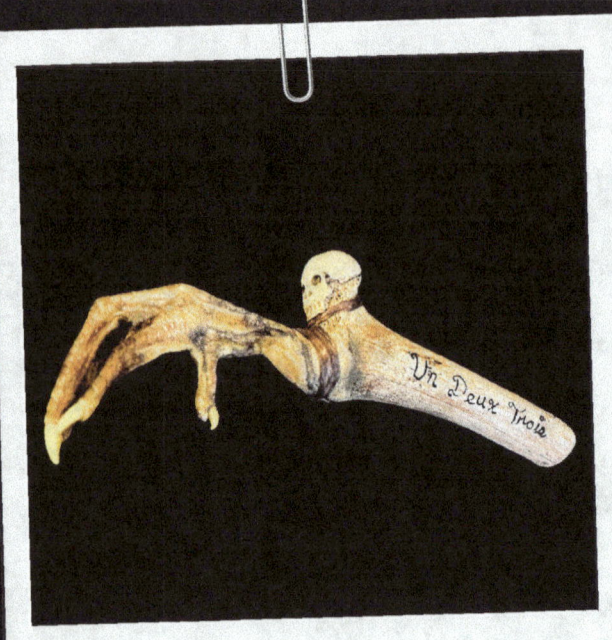

THE WHISTLE:

The whistle's body is made of bone, with a bird's foot attached to the front.

Above the foot is a skull carved into the bone.

The words "One, Two, Three" are also carved (in French) on the side of the whistle.

Good evening Satori and Cody,

Please forgive me for writing to you in my language. I can speak English much better than I can write, so please forgive me. I hope you can translate well. I really like ghosts and the supernatural, that's how I located your show on the internet and discovered your amazing museum. I have something that was given to me by my mother. My mother told me that her grandmother was a practicing witch here when she was alive. My mother tells me that she grew up with stories from her mother about how her grandmother was part of a witch group that cast spells to help people and bless those who perform evil in her eyes.

My mother doesn't remember her grandmother, but always heard stories from her mother.

After she passed away, most of her witch stuff was passed down to her witch circle group.

When the pandemic hit the world in 2020, my mother remembered a story she had been told when she was younger about her grandmother. As the story was told to me, in the early I900s, there was another type of pandemic or disease that was spread quickly by poultry. My mother tells me that her grandmother and other witches would cast spells to ward off illness. Part of the spell was blowing whistles that they made. My mother was told that they looked like a bone with a bird leg attached to it, but my mother never actually saw it.

A few months ago, my mother was going through old boxes at my grandmother's house and she actually found one of the whistles. I thought it was the coolest thing that she found something that belonged to her grandmother and that she had heard about growing up.

She ended up giving it to me and I replaced the mouthpiece because the old one was falling apart and I wanted to hear what it sounded like.

When I finally blew it, my mom and I got complete chills and haven't had it since. Others who have heard the whistle have felt sick and very anxious. I think it will have negative effects on individuals because it was only designed with one person's intention to use it.

I asked my mom if she cared if I gave you the whistle, and she loved the idea because it would be in a safe place so it wouldn't hurt people and it would tell a great story.

Would you like to accept this donation?

Thank you so much,

Genevieve Dupont

Genevieve Dupont

𝔇𝔞𝔦𝔩𝔶 𝔗𝔯𝔦𝔟𝔲𝔫𝔢

VOL. 13, NO. 8 ✳ *SPECIAL EDITION* ✳ *10 OCTOBER 1918*

SPANISH FLU RAVAGES FRANCE AMID GLOBAL PANDEMIC

THOUSANDS DEAD IN UNSTOPPABLE SPANISH FLU EPIDEMIC

France is in the grip of the deadly Spanish Flu, a global pandemic that has claimed tens of thousands of lives nationwide and millions worldwide. First appearing in the spring of 1918, the virus has spread rapidly, exacerbated by the movement of troops and refugees during World War I.

The flu is lethal, striking young, healthy adults with severe symptoms that often lead to pneumonia and death within days. Cities like Paris have imposed restrictions on public gatherings, while hospitals are overwhelmed with patients and shortages of medicine.

The pandemic has paralyzed much of the country, forcing businesses, schools, and factories to close. Rural areas and urban centers alike are reporting mass fatalities, leaving communities devastated. By 1920, France is expected to have lost over 400,000 citizens to the disease.

As the nation mourns, the pandemic underscores the urgent need for medical research and public health reforms to prevent such tragedies in the future.

1918

Gauze Mask to Halt Spread of Plague

This image captures the newly designed mask adopted by the Red Cross to combat the spread of Spanish influenza in the United States. It features a Red Cross worker wearing the mask while actively engaged in its production. These masks are specifically designed to prevent the inhalation and exhalation of influenza germs, aiding in the effort to contain the pandemic.

1894 - 1901

POULTRY FARMS ACROSS EUROPE DEVASTATED

A MYSTERIOUS AND DEADLY DISEASE, REFERRED TO AS "FOWL PLAGUE," IS SWEEPING THROUGH POULTRY FARMS ACROSS EUROPE, LEAVING DEVASTATION IN ITS WAKE.

AUTHORITIES ARE STRUGGLING TO CONTAIN THE SPREAD OF THE DISEASE.

Outbreaks around that time period...

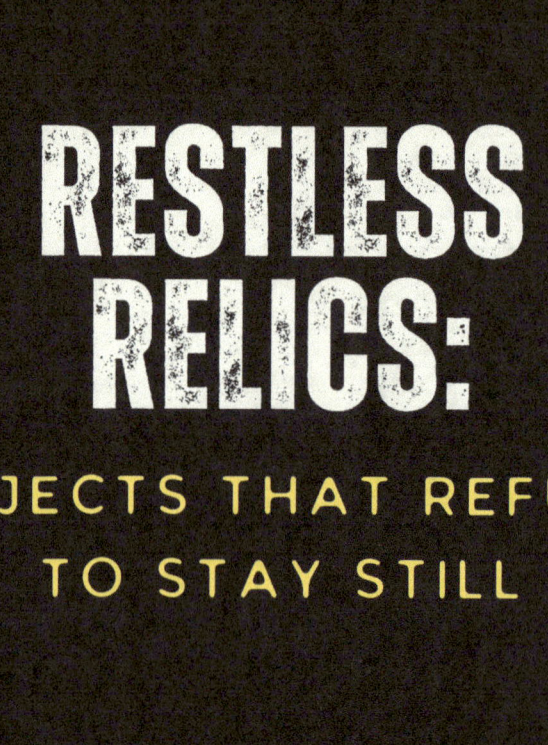

RESTLESS RELICS:

OBJECTS THAT REFUSE
TO STAY STILL

POSSIBLE REASONS WHY OBJECTS MAY MOVE ON THEIR OWN

* Spirit Attachment: A spirit or entity tied to an object may manipulate it to communicate, or assert its presence.

* Energy Transfer: An object may absorb and releases energy from its environment, possibly causing slight movements or shifts.

* Repetitive Memory: An object may "reenact" movements tied to its past, such as being knocked over, or handled in a significant moment.

* Symbolic Warning: A movement may serve as a signal or omen, often tied to the object's history, or the owner's actions.

FUN FACT:
One day, we entered the museum to find that most of the dolls were either turned backwards to face the wall, or their heads were spun around. We still have no idea how this happened.

Of all the strange phenomena associated with haunted objects, perhaps the most unnerving is movement. Imagine walking past a display or exhibit, glancing back, and realizing an object is now in a different position. Or setting down a piece of jewelry, only to find it in another room hours later. Take a pile of toys as another example, seemingly changing places every time you leave and enter a room. For many, the first sight of a haunted object moving is a chilling reminder that these items may not be as inanimate as they seem.

Over the years, countless visitors to our museum exhibitions and lectures have witnessed objects shifting on their own. Sometimes, it's a matter of inches: a description sign that slowly creeps its way off of a shelf, a pen rolling on its own. Other times, the movement is more pronounced, almost deliberate, as if the object is attempting to reach out to someone in particular. We have heard dozens of gasps and whispers as guests report seeing a faint, nearly imperceptible shift in a piece's position. And occasionally, we have encountered an object so restless that it must be carefully stored away, removed from public view entirely.

There are many theories about why haunted objects move. Paranormal researchers have long debated whether this is the work of a spirit attached to the item, or if it's due to an energy "imprint." This is a residual force left behind by a previous owner or encounter. In some cases, the object involved once belonged to someone deeply attached to it. That attachment, even after death, sometimes seems to linger.

One hypothesis suggests that strong emotions—grief, love, anger, can "charge" an object, imprinting it with energy that persists beyond the physical life of its owner. This energy may not always be conscious or directed, but may result in movements that mimic the owner's former interactions with the item.

Another theory is that certain objects serve as "anchors" for a spirit —whether willingly or due to unfinished business. Spirits who are unable to move on are theorized by some to be drawn to particular objects, unable to leave it behind even in death. These spirits may manifest by manipulating the item in an attempt to communicate, or seek out attention.

These types of paranormal stories aren't just isolated incidents— they're accounts from thousands of people, skeptics and believers alike, who've experienced the impossible. Many come to the museum doubtful, expecting only to hear eerie tales, and see dusty relics. But in the event that they witness movement—a slight tilt, a turn, the faint sense of being watched—skepticism often gives way to wonder, or fear.

While the scientific community remains cautious, the sheer volume of these accounts has been hard to dismiss. For every recorded video, for every trembling witness who stares in disbelief, there's a growing sense that haunted objects may indeed carry traces of their former owners' lives. We can only guess at what forces may be at work, and what emotions or energies truly animate these objects. But when something moves before your eyes, when it reaches out from beyond the realm of explanation, the sense of paranormal mystery is undeniable.

As we continue to study haunted objects, we remain vigilant, prepared for what the next piece may reveal. In a world of unexplained movements and hidden answers, every haunted object holds its own story—waiting to come alive once more.

EYE KNOW WHAT YOU DID

In the heart of Montana, a home sat as it had for decades. Its creaking floors and mature walls told stories of time gone by, a symbol of all the memories that had been made within it.

For Kelly Arnold, her grandparents had always been the soul of the house. Her grandfather, a hard working yet loving man, had always filled the home with laughter and warmth, even as his health waned in his final years. When he passed away in August of 2022, the home felt different, it was so much quieter. His belongings, too, were reminders of a man who had left a deep impression on the world, and all who truly knew him. Among these belongings was an item that seemed ordinary for him, but strange to many others. A prosthetic eye, small and brown, one of a few he had kept over the years. This eye, however, was his favorite.

At first, after his passing, the family paid little attention to the prosthetic eyes. It had sat untouched in his room, a silent relic of his life. His other possessions were carefully sorted, some boxed away, others passed on to new homes. When the day of the funeral finally came, the family chose one of his artificial eyes to be buried with him, a gesture that was meant to ensure he was laid to rest with a special part of who he was.

But almost immediately after his burial, the home began to change.

It started subtly. The remaining eye on the dresser, once forgotten, was no longer in the position that they had originally left it. Kelly noticed that it had shifted slightly forward, as though it had been placed intentionally to face the doorway. The first occurance she had dismissed as a coincidence. The movement soon grew bolder, almost deliberate, as though it was meant to send a clear message.

Then came the sounds. During quiet periods, they would begin to hear the unmistakable creak of hardwood floors in grandpa Joe's room. The sounds within the room grew louder and more consistent. It was almost as if he was still alive, and roaming around in his usual routine. Then came the lights. On multiple occasions, the family would notice that the lamp, located in the grandparents room, would be turned on with no logical explanation.

Kelly's grandmother Doris, though a bit more hesitant to voice her thoughts, began to notice the unexplainable as well. One evening, as Doris was at home, a familiar scent hit her. It smelt exactly like her late husband's aftershave, faint but unmistakable. It was a smell she hadn't encountered since before his passing. It was like he was standing in the room with her, but she just couldn't see him.

At first, the family found comfort in these signs, believing they were small reminders that he was still with them. But as the activity grew, so did their unease. The eye seemed to be at the center of it all, moving again and again, as though calling out to be noticed. Lights turning on were strangely located by the eye, almost acting as a spotlight. The traveling sounds and smells, practically calling for the family's attention. It wasn't long before the family began to wonder if they had made a mistake. Had they buried him with the wrong eye? Was his spirit trying to tell them that they had overlooked something so deeply personal?

The home, once a place of peace, now carried an air of uncertainty. The weight of their possible mistake, or what they believed to be a mistake, pressed on them daily. Kelly's grandmother, once unshakable, began to grow fearful of the eye, as she felt that her husband was using it to express his upset from the other side. Desperate for answers, Kelly sent an email to the museum seeking help.

What followed was a conversation that would set the stage for one of our most unusual cases. Kelly shared her story in detail. Her words carried a mix of guilt, confusion, and hope. Guilt for what they might have done wrong, confusion over the events that had followed, and hope that perhaps by entrusting the eye to the museum, her grandfather's spirit might find attention if needed, and peace.

For us, the case was compelling, yet shrouded in mystery. Was this truly a message from beyond, a grandfather reaching out to correct a small but meaningful oversight? Or was the family's belief in their mistake amplifying occurrences into something extraordinary?

This is Case #100522, Eye Know What You Did.

CASE FILE

NAME: EYE KNOW WHAT YOU DID

CASE#: 100522

DATE: October 5, 2022

CASE #: 100522 - Eye Know What You Did...

CLIENT NAME: Kelly Arnold
ALL OCCUPANTS AT LOCATION: Kelly (Client), Doris (Client's Grandmother), Julie (Client's Mother)
DATE OF CASE: August - October of 2022
DATE CLIENT OBTAINED OBJECT: August of 2022
CLIENT LOCATION: Montana
LOCATION OBTAINED: (Grandfather) Joe's Room
OBJECT MANUFACTURE ORIGIN: Unknown

POINT OF CONTACT
EMAIL SENT TO PARANORMAL COUPLE ACCOUNT:
From: ***************@email.com
Date: October 5, 2022 at 09:27:02 PM EST
To: contact@paranormalcouple.com
Subject: NEED HELP

HI Satori and Cody,

I want to send you my grandfather's eye, what is the address? Thank you!

Kelly

EMAIL REPLY SENT FROM PARANORMAL COUPLE ACCOUNT:
To: **************@email.com
Date: October 5, 2022 at 11:18:53 PM EST
From: contact@paranormalcouple.com
Subject: RE: NEED HELP

Hey Kelly!

Hope all is going well! We would love to have more information about the item, as well as a description of any activity that has occurred. We would also like to set up a phone call to ask some questions about your experiences. That would be very helpful for the museum!
Please let us know what your schedule looks like.

Talk soon,
Cody & Satori

EMAIL REPLY SENT TO PARANORMAL COUPLE ACCOUNT:
From: **************@email.com
Date: October 6, 2022 at 07:12:40 PM EST
To: contact@paranormalcouple.com
Subject: NEED HELP

Hello Paranormal Couple,
Ya sure I can! Sorry that I didn't give more information in my first message. I didn't want to write it out and go into detail if you had no interest in having it.
The eye belonged to my grandfather Joe. If I remember correctly, he had 3 or 4 of them in case he lost one or something. They obviously all looked identical, but for some reason he had a favorite eye that he would always wear. I think it may have been more comfortable for him or something.
To get to the point, by the end of his life he had somehow lost all but 2 of them. When he was in his final days, he did not wear his eye anymore so it was placed with the other one he had.

When he did pass, we had the funeral home put in one of the last 2 eyes. All of that is fine, but the weird stuff started to happen after he was buried. We honestly think all of this paranormal activity that started up is our fault. We think that we gave the funeral home the wrong eye to bury him in. Again, they looked identical to us, but one of them was his favorite, and we think that we buried him with the wrong one and his actual favorite is the one that keeps moving in his room.

We of course have no use for it and thought we would send it to you both after watching one of your live videos. We feel really comfortable with you both owning it because you both seem so kind and respectful to your other artifacts.

We are fine with you sharing this story publicly, but we just ask / wish that you not share our name because the local town folks may think differently of us if they get word of this. I hope you both understand. But we really are thankful that you both are willing to take my grandfather's eye. The activity seemed to slow down after we put it in a little box, but not completely. We pray that the activity will stop completely after it is gone.

Either way we know it will be in a good home / museum. Maybe we can come up and visit it someday. Thank you.

If you need any more info or questions, let me know. Thanks.

Kelly

PRELIMINARY PHONE INTERVIEW

PHONE INTERVIEW BY: Cody Ray DesBiens & Satori Hawes
DATE: Saturday - October 8 2022
CLIENT NAME: Kelly Arnold
PHONE NUMBER: ***-***-****
EMAIL: **************@email.com

DESCRIPTION OF OBJECT IN QUESTION:

- Small prosthetic eye.
- Brown in color.
- Eye is placed in a small, colorful, trunk box.

HOW WAS THE OBJECT OBTAINED:

- Our client (Kelly) states that she and her mother (Julie) have lived with her grandparents (Doris and Joe) for most of her life.
- Recently, Kelly's grandfather had unfortunately passed away.
- After his passing, all of his belongings were left to his family.
- Among these belongings were two of his remaining prosthetic eyes.
- He had lost one of his eyes in an accident while working on his farm at a younger age. Due to this, he had multiple prosthetic eyes that he would use. One eye was his favorite, however.
- After his passing, the family placed one of the eyes with Joe, and left the other one in the same spot that they had found it in. This soon changed once activity started.

WHY DO YOU THINK THE OBJECT IS THE CAUSE OF THE PARANORMAL ACTIVITY:

- Kelly states that right after her grandfather was buried, activity started.
- When Kelly and her family began to enter Joe's room, they noticed that things would shift and change on their own.
- The entire household has never experienced paranormal activity like this before the grandfather's burial.
- Kelly expresses that "it's like someone flipped on the light here from the other side."

HOW LONG HAVE YOU BEEN AT THIS LOCATION?:

- The Arnold family has lived on this property for multiple decades.
- The farmhouse was built by Joe, and before the house was constructed, there was a small cabin on the property that Joe was born in. Each generation has lived on the property, or in the same house since that day.

UNEXPLAINED TEMPERATURE CHANGES:

- The grandmother (Doris) has reported that she has felt colder in recent weeks while in her home and bedroom (which she used to share with Joe).

UNEXPLAINED ANOMALIES WITH ELECTRICAL DEVICES:
- Kelly states that the lamp on her grandfather's dresser has been found turned on mysteriously on two occasions.
- She expresses that no one has touched the lamp, even when her grandfather was alive. Only her grandfather would.
- He was the one that would turn it on and off while he was getting ready for the day.
- It is also important to note that this is the same dresser that the eye has been sitting on.

UNEXPLAINED ILLNESS:
- None Reported.

UNEXPLAINED ODORS:
- Kelly's grandmother stated last week that she had noticed the scent of her late husband's aftershave upon entering her bedroom.
- She expressed that she hadn't smelled that scent since before his passing.

MANIPULATION OF OBJECTS:
- On multiple occasions, Kelly and her family have found the eye moved on top of the dresser.
- Twice now they have walked into Joe's room and found the eye positioned forward. Its new position was giving the appearance of looking towards the entrance of the bedroom.
- Kelly immediately got freaked out by this when she found it the second time.
- The first time it happened, she brushed it off, but the second occurance gave her certainty that no one (living) had moved the eye.
- It was at this point that the family started to conclude that they may have buried grandpa with the wrong eye, which is why he was moving the eye in their home.

APPARITIONS/VISUAL ANOMALIES:
- None Reported.

UNEXPLAINED VOICES:

- None Reported.

UNEXPLAINED SOUNDS:

- Multiple sounds have started to occur over the past week or so.
- It all seems to be centered around Joe's room.
- Nothing paranormal has ever occurred in any other areas of the home.
- Kelly states that she has "heard the hardwood floor boards creek several times like a person was standing there shifting their weight."
- Because of these experiences with the sounds, and the eye moving, Kelly has put the eye in a small trinket box. She has moved it to the spare room to see if there was a change.
- She states that since she has done that, "experiences have died down a lot, but not completely."

PHYSICAL CONTACT:

- None Reported.

DESIRED RESULT / OUTCOME:

- Kelly and her family just want to live in peace.
- The entire Arnold family knows that the spirit of Joe is behind the activity, and that it is nothing negative, but they still feel terrible that they may have made a mistake when choosing the prosthetic eye.
- Jokingly, Kelly states that her family hopes that by donating the eye to the museum, that it will "possibly make grandpa happy that he is getting attention."
- She also stated that her grandmother (Doris) is afraid of the dark, and when she witnesses things herself, it freaks her out.
- Kelly also states that Doris is afraid of her husband possibly being upset, and is terrified of the eye due to this idea.
- Lastly, the family expressed that they have many other things that belonged to grandpa to remember him by. "We know it will be safe with you both and it will be well taken care of."

INVESTIGATOR NOTES:
- Kelly seems to be one step ahead of us by placing the eye in a box, and moving it to another, less used room.
- We always recommend doing this with "problematic items" to target if the activity is truly surrounding the object.
- According to the client, it seems that activity in her grandfather's bedroom diminished greatly after removing the item, which is a good sign that activity is mostly surrounding the object.
- We have instructed Kelly on the proper steps in order to send the item to the museum, and we await its arrival.

NOTES:

DATE OF ENTRY TO MUSEUM: Thursday - October 13, 2022
- Today, we received the item from Kelly and her family in the mail.
- We opened the small box, exposing the eye, and placed it on a table within the quarantine room for observation.
- We do not expect much to happen with this item due to the fact that the activity was seemingly directed at the family. It could have been a message telling them that they may have chosen the wrong eye.
- With that being said, we do not know what may or may not occur over the next week in quarantine.

CLIENT FOLLOW UP: Sunday - October 23, 2022
- Satori and I were able to reach our client Kelly.
- All in all they are at peace, and the home seems like it is back to normal again activity-wise.
- The client's grandmother (Doris) is not afraid of the dark as much anymore with the addition of a light that Kelly purchased for her.
- The family states that activity has stopped, but they know that "grandpa is still here watching over things."

CLIENT FOLLOW UP: January, 2025
- Contact has been made with Kelly on multiple occasions since our previous follow up in 2022
- Kelly has kept us updated on her family, and states that all is still peaceful after the item's donation.

THE CLICKING BALLET

Brigham City, Utah, is a town where life flows quietly, framed by the majestic Wasatch Mountains and painted with the subtle hues of small-town charm. For Erin and Noah Martin, it was the perfect place to build their lives together, a home that radiated warmth, love, and the rhythm of the ordinary. Over two decades, the couple had never experienced anything that would make them question the world they thought they knew. But in the final days of December 2022, the Martins' steady life unraveled into a tangle of chaos, fear, confusion, and the paranormal.

It began innocently enough. Erin and Noah often visited yard sales, enjoying the hunt for something special. One morning, they decided to stop by a local church sale on a whim. The church, bustling with people and the warmth of the holiday season, offered tables of knickknacks, books, and other forgotten treasures. While Erin casually browsed, Noah's attention was drawn almost immediately towards a small statue. It was seemingly a ballerina, poised delicately on a stone base, her arm arched in an elegant frame over her head.

Noah couldn't explain why the figure caught his eye. He only knew that he had to bring it home. Their granddaughter, Abigail, a young girl with an undeniable passion for ballet, would surely love it. As he picked up the statue, a strange sensation began to prickle his skin. The item was unusually warm, almost as if it had been sitting in the sun. He glanced around the church hall, but saw no reason for the statue's mysterious heat. Shrugging it off as nothing, he carried the item to the cashier, paid a few dollars, and tucked the ballerina under his arm.

As the couple drove home, the warmth of the statue faded. It was soon replaced by something else, an odd feeling, hard to name but impossible to ignore. A sense of heaviness settled over Noah, like a shadow lingering out of sight. Erin noticed his unease, but when she asked about it, he waved it off. After all, how could a tiny statue cause such a random shift in his mood?

That Christmas, the ballerina became part of their granddaughter's gifts. The young girl was delighted, placing it on the dresser in the guest room at her grandparents' house, where she often stayed on weekends. But from the moment the statue entered their home, the Martins began to notice changes, subtle at first, but increasingly disturbing.

The guest room grew unnaturally cold, as though the warmth of their central heating refused to penetrate its walls. No matter how high the thermostat was set, their granddaughter needed extra blankets to fight off the chill. Then there were the lightbulbs. Within days of the ballerina's arrival, three separate bulbs in the room shattered without any warning. They broke one after the other, as though something unseen was rejecting their light.

And then the sound started. At first, it was faint, a soft clicking noise, like the crackle of old wood. Their granddaughter Abigail heard it most often during the nights she stayed over, but soon, Erin and Noah noticed it too. It was always coming from the guest room, echoing through the stillness of the house.

The breaking point came late one night when their granddaughter awoke to the clicking sound once again. It was louder now, sharper, and impossible to ignore. Nervous, but curious, Abigail turned on her bedside lamp and froze. In the dim light, she saw the ballerina moving, not dancing, but shifting unnaturally. Each click corresponded to a sudden jerk of its limbs. Its arms and legs were twisting into grotesque new positions. Terrified, she screamed, bringing Erin and Noah running.

When they entered the room, they were hit with an overwhelming stench of sulfur. The ballerina sat still and lifeless on the dresser, as if nothing happened. But the fear in their granddaughter's eyes was undeniable, and the cold dread creeping up Erin's spine told her that something was very, very wrong.

From that night on, the disturbances grew worse. Noah moved the ballerina into the basement, hoping to ease his granddaughter's fears, but the clicking was still occurring. While returning upstairs, a low rumbling sound filled the house. It was as though something heavy had shifted below. When Noah reached the basement, he was startled to find his large rolling toolbox, something far too heavy to just move around, blocking the view of the statue.

Erin and Noah knew that they could no longer handle the situation on their own. Their granddaughter was too scared to visit. Their once comforting home had turned into a source of family fear. Desperate for answers, and a way to reclaim their peace, they reached out to the museum.

Their email was straightforward and laced with urgency. Unbeknownst to Erin and Noah, their plea would open the door to one of the strangest, and most unnerving cases in our archive.

This is Case #011923, The Clicking Ballet.

WHAT IS A COLD SPOT?

Current theories behind cold spots are based on the idea that spirits require energy to manifest. According to this idea, when a spirit attempts to appear, move objects, or interact with the physical world, it draws energy from its surroundings. This energy intake can lead to a noticeable drop in temperature, creating what we call a cold spot.

INVESTIGATING A COLD SPOT:

• Use thermal cameras or temperature sensors to document changes.

• Check for natural explanations such as drafts, open vents, or temperature differences between rooms.

• See if the cold spot moves or responds to questions, which could indicate intelligent interaction.

INFRARED THERMOMETER

This handheld device measures surface temperature. It provides quick, non-contact temperature readings. This makes it an ideal tool for investigations where sudden temperature fluctuations need to be documented.

CASE FILE

THE PARANORMAL COMPLEX
HAUNTED MUSEUM OF
OF ALL THE ODDITIES AND CURIOSITIES

NAME: THE CLICKING BALLET

CASE#: 011923

DATE: January 19, 2023

CLIENT NAME: Erin and Noah Martin
ALL OCCUPANTS AT LOCATION: Erin (client), Noah (Husband), Abigail (Granddaughter) (visits a few days a week)
DATE OF CASE: December 2022 / January 2023
DATE CLIENT OBTAINED OBJECT: December 2022
CLIENT LOCATION: Brigham City, Utah
LOCATION OBTAINED: Church Yard Sale
OBJECT MANUFACTURE ORIGIN: Unknown. Possibly handmade by an artist.

POINT OF CONTACT
EMAIL SENT TO PARANORMAL COUPLE ACCOUNT:
From: ***************@email.com
Date: January 19, 2023 at 4:08:41 PM EST
To: contact@paranormalcouple.com
Subject: I HAVE A HAUNTED OBJECT

Dear Satori and Cody,
I hope you both are having a good start to your New Year. My name is Erin Martin and my husband's name is Noah.
I am reaching out for some assistance.
Noah purchased a small ballerina statue from a local church sale for our granddaughter Abigail as a Christmas gift. She loves ballet and has been dancing for a few years now.
After Christmas, she put the doll in her room here at our house and some really weird and creepy things began to occur that have been really scaring her.
We would love to explain more over a telephone call possibly. Thank you for your time.
Respectfully,
Mr. & Mrs. Martin

PRELIMINARY PHONE INTERVIEW

PHONE INTERVIEW BY: Cody Ray DesBiens & SatoriHawes
DATE: Saturday - January 21, 2023
CLIENT NAME: Erin Martin
PHONE NUMBER: ***-***-****
EMAIL: **************@email.com

DESCRIPTION OF OBJECT IN QUESTION:
- Metal ballerina statue. Mounted to stone.
- Approximately six inches in height.

HOW WAS THE OBJECT OBTAINED:
- During the beginning of last month (December 2022), the client (Erin) and her husband (Noah) decided to stop in at a Church yard sale.
- Erin stated that they did not belong to this church, but they had driven by it on several occasions and thought that they would drop in to look around.
- Upon walking into the church, Noah was immediately drawn to this particular statue.
- He states that he "noticed right away that it was a ballerina, and I knew I had to get it for little Abigail."
- He grabbed the statue and said that it oddly felt "really hot," like it was sitting in the sun, or near a fire. He looked around and didn't see anything abnormal, so he kept walking.
- They both looked around for a little longer before deciding to pay for the statue, and head out.
- Noah expressed that on the way home, "something just felt different."

HOW LONG HAVE YOU BEEN AT THIS LOCATION?:
- Noah purchased the home (brand new) in 2002.
- Before living in this home, they had lived in a condominium building a few towns over.
- They state that nothing paranormal has ever happened at either location.

WHY DO YOU THINK THE OBJECT IS THE CAUSE OF THE PARANORMAL ACTIVITY:

- Erin and Noah both state that activity only began days after the statute was brought into their home.
- They express that they have lived in the same home for over twenty years, and there has never been any paranormal activity.
- They claim that "it was a drastic emotional change that we had never experienced before, and we didn't understand why it was happening."

UNEXPLAINED TEMPERATURE CHANGES:

- Once the client's granddaughter (Abigail) received the gift, it was placed on top of a dresser in her room.
- Erin states, "ever since she put the statue in that room, it has been frigid."
- She also states that it has gotten so cold in that room, that Abigail has needed multiple extra blankets.
- For some reason the heating system in the home refuses to adjust the temperature in that room, but the rest of the home is fine.

UNEXPLAINED ANOMALIES WITH ELECTRICAL DEVICES:

- Erin and Noah state that the only abnormal electrical disturbance that has repeatedly occurred concerns the light bulbs in Abigail's room.
- There have been three different instances in which light bulbs have blown out in front of someone with no explanation.
- Noah also states that the instances came from two different lamps. This eliminates the possibility of the lamp itself being the cause.

UNEXPLAINED ILLNESS:

- On multiple different occasions, Erin states that both her and Noah have experienced horrible headaches.
- According to Erin, most of the headaches have occurred directly before or after a paranormal encounter.

MANIPULATION OF OBJECTS:

- Erin states that this has been incredibly unnerving for all of them, but primarily Abigail.
- The past few nights that Abigail has slept over at her grandparents home, she has heard a clicking sound start up.
- Erin states that the only thing that Abigail can compare it to is someone cracking their knuckles.
- In the first few instances of this, she didn't know what it was, and just ignored it.
- During this latest occurrence, Abigail decided to turn the light on. This turned out to be the worst decision that she could have made.
- Once her eyes adjusted to the light, she looked over and watched the ballerina move in a "disturbing way."
- Abigail states that every time there was a click, she would witness one of the arms or legs of the statue change position quickly with no logical explanation.
- "It was one of those things that felt impossible to witness" according to Erin.
- Abigail screamed, alerting her grandparents. The statue was then covered up.

UNEXPLAINED ODORS:

- When Abigail screamed, Erin and Noah both woke up and ran into her room.
- Upon entering the room, they smelled what they described as "a thousand matches being lit at once. This overwhelming smell of sulfur, no smoke but just the smell."
- The horrible headaches appeared soon after.
- Noah quickly looked around the room while Erin comforted Abigail.
- Nothing abnormal was found to their surprise.

UNEXPLAINED SOUNDS:

- After the clicking event, Abigail begged her grandparents to take the statue out of her room.
- Noah ended up placing it in the basement of their home.

- As he was coming up the stairs he heard the clicking sound begin, and then a huge rumble which startled the entire family.
- Erin immediately thought that Noah had taken a fall down the stairs.
- After assuring that he was okay, Noah turned around and went back downstairs to see what happened.
- To his astonishment, his large rolling tool chest had been pushed into the middle of the floor, blocking his view to the statue.
- This really freaked him out because he knows how heavy that toolbox is, and how hard it is to move.

UNEXPLAINED VOICES:
- Since the statue has been in the basement, mumbling sounds have been heard by both Erin and Noah.
- They describe the sound as a "television has been left on," but there is no TV in the basement.
- As soon as they open the door to check on the sound, the mumbling stops.
- They have found no explanation.

APPARITIONS/VISUAL ANOMALIES:
- Erin and Noah decided to contact the museum after their most recent experience.
- A few nights ago, they were preparing dinner for just the two of them, as they were alone without their granddaughter.
- They began to hear the sound of the mumbling coming from the basement, so they decided to open the door (and leave it open) to see if the noise would continue, or stop.
- A few moments later, they both began to feel a headache coming on. The smell of sulfur filled the air, and they then witnessed a tall dark shadow figure dart across the hall near the basement door.
- They stated that at this point they began to pray, and eventually got the courage to close the basement door once again.
- They contacted the museum that night.

PHYSICAL CONTACT:
- None Reported.

DESIRED RESULT / OUTCOME:
- Abigail is scared to visit her grandparents after the clicking incident.
- Noah regrets purchasing the item, and wishes that he never had.
- At this point, they just want everything to go back to the way it was before the statue was brought into their home.
- The most important thing to them is that their granddaughter feels comfortable visiting, and sleeping over.

INVESTIGATOR NOTES:
- We have instructed Mr. & Mrs. Martin on how to ship the statue to the museum.
- Since the granddaughter is old enough to understand what is happening, we think that it is important to include her in the process of shipping the statue.
- This will reassure her that the statue has been removed from the home, and that this is the first step of things going back to the way they were.

NOTES:

DATE OF ENTRY TO MUSEUM: Monday - January 30, 2023
- Today, we received the statue in the mail.
- We have placed it on a small table within the quarantine room.
- We have also put some baby powder around it to see if there is any slight movement that is not noticeable on camera.

IMPORTANT UPDATE: Friday - February 3, 2023
- This evening, Satori and I (Cody) opened the quarantine room door to check on the statue, and we were immediately hit in the face with the smell of sulfur. This is what the clients described.
- We found no normal explanation as to why this could happen.
- The statue's stone platform does not give off a smell of sulfur when close by. Neither does the statue itself. Eliminating the stone and metal composition as possible culprits.

IMPORTANT UPDATE: Sunday - February 5, 2023

- Today, I (Cody) went to check the quarantine camera on my phone, when I noticed that it was turned off.
- Upon reviewing the footage, the camera flashed on and off rapidly until it finally shut off for good.
- This could have a normal explanation, but I have not witnessed this happen in the past.
- I replaced the camera, and all seems to be working well at this point.

CLIENT FOLLOW UP: Saturday - February 11, 2023 - PHONE CALL

- Today, we were able to reach our client (Erin) and her husband (Noah) over the phone.
- One immediately good sign is that we heard their granddaughter (Abigail) in the background of the call.
- The clients both expressed how happy they were now that whatever was in their house is gone.
- They stated that they don't talk about the former experiences in the house anymore, especially around Abigail.
- Abigail seems to be happy, and has now returned to the routine of sleeping over every week.

JOLENE

Jean Ross had always considered herself a practical person. As a daycare owner, she was used to handling chaos with a sort of calm efficiency, from frenzied toddlers to tantrums over missing toys. So when Jean purchased a home in Connecticut, and found a large handmade clown doll left behind in the attic, she didn't think much of it. The doll, with its colorful outfit, was quite peculiar but rather harmless, or so it seemed. Nicknamed "Jolene" by Jean's family, the doll was left to gather dust in the attic, little more than a forgotten object of the home's past.

But as months passed, Jolene's story began to take shape, and it was one Jean could have never anticipated.

By early 2018, Jean's daycare had expanded from her home to a new standalone facility within the same town. With the move, she decided to bring Jolene along as a useful addition to the space. It was an innocent gesture, a genuine attempt to add some charm to the playroom. To Jean's surprise, the children were immediately drawn to the doll. They clung to Jolene's hands and feet, whispering to her as if she could respond. Staff chalked it up to the creativity of childhood imagination, but there was something unsettling about the way these children interacted with the doll. The exchanges seemed as though Jolene was more than just a lifeless toy.

Then the real incidents began.

At first, they were easy to dismiss: toys malfunctioning, Jolene oddly found a few feet away from her designated chair in the morning. But the doll's presence quickly became a source of fear. The children, once enjoying Jolene's presence, began crying uncontrollably. They began claiming that Jolene was calling them cruel names. The staff initially brushed off the children's complaints, until one by one, they too became uneasy. The doll would begin to appear in different positions overnight, surrounded by toys as if it had been alive and playing on its own. Jean, the only individual with a key to the building, knew that no one could have gained inside access to the building in order to move the doll. There it was, however, night after night, defying all logical explanation.

Jean began to feel the toll of Jolene's presence in ways that she couldn't ignore. Nights became restless, as she found herself lying awake, replaying the day's strange events. Her once unshakable confidence, and level headed attitude, soon began to erode under the weight of both the doll's mysterious movements, and the children's mounting fear. Even when she was away from the daycare, Jean couldn't escape the creeping sense of unease that seemed to consistently linger. It was as if Jolene's influence extended far beyond the walls of the building.

Jean was finally at her breaking point. The daycare had become a source of dread. Its cheerful energy was now replaced with a heavy, suffocating atmosphere. The children seemed noticeably happier when the doll was locked away, but its mere presence in the building still felt oppressive. Jean couldn't bring herself to even touch Jolene anymore, and that is when she reached out to the museum. She practically begged us to remove the doll, vowing never to set foot in the daycare again until it was gone.

Our experiences within this investigation would begin to test our own beliefs about the unexplained. From the moment Jolene was moved to the museum, strange phenomena seemed to follow.

This is Case #030318, the story of Jolene, a harmless-looking clown doll that became the center of a chilling mystery. This is the story of a woman who sought only to create a safe, happy environment for children, but instead found herself at the mercy of an entity that she could neither understand nor control.

Some objects carry memories. Others carry something deeper. Sometimes, objects refuse to be forgotten. Jolene, however, demands to be remembered.

CASE FILE

NAME: JOLENE

CASE#: 030318

DATE: March 3, 2018

CLIENT NAME: Jean Ross
ALL OCCUPANTS AT LOCATION: Jean (Daycare Owner), 4 Staff members, multiple children
DATE OF CASE: Winter / Spring of 2017-2018
DATE CLIENT OBTAINED OBJECT: 2017
CLIENT LOCATION: Connecticut
LOCATION OBTAINED: Found in new home
OBJECT MANUFACTURE ORIGIN: Handmade

POINT OF CONTACT
MESSAGE SENT TO CODY VIA SOCIAL MEDIA:
DATE: Saturday - February 24, 2018

TAYLOR: Hey! Great interview last night! My mom's boss is having some issues at her work with a doll. Can I tell her to contact you?

CODY: Hi! Thanks for listening! Yes! Absolutely you can tell her to contact me. If she wants, she can give me a call at ***-***-****.

TAYLOR: Okay will do! Thank you!

PHONE INTERVIEW BY: Cody Ray DesBiens
DATE: March 3, 2018
CLIENT NAME: Jean Ross
PHONE NUMBER: ***-***-****
EMAIL: **********@email.com

DESCRIPTION OF OBJECT IN QUESTION:

- Large stuffed clown doll.
- Approximately 4 feet in length.
- Decorated with multiple colored fabric.
- Believed to be handmade.

HOW WAS THE OBJECT OBTAINED:

- When the client (Jean) purchased her new home in 2017, the doll was left behind by the previous owners.
- Jean's family nicknamed the doll "Jolene," and she stayed in the attic until being moved to her current location in early 2018.

WHY DO YOU THINK THE OBJECT IS THE CAUSE OF THE PARANORMAL ACTIVITY:

- Jean is the owner of a daycare facility in Connecticut.
- She brought the doll into the building, and immediately, the children were drawn to it in "what seemed like a loving way."

HOW LONG HAVE YOU BEEN AT THIS LOCATION?:

- Jean moved into her current house in 2017.
- The daycare started in Jean's home shortly after moving in.
- Jean then moved the daycare into its current building about six months later.
- In January of 2018, Jolene was brought into the facility.

UNEXPLAINED TEMPERATURE CHANGES:

- None Reported.

UNEXPLAINED ANOMALIES WITH ELECTRICAL DEVICES:

- Jean states that there have been some battery operated toys that have "acting strange" since the doll was brought into the facility.
- These toys have never malfunctioned, and looking back, Jean states that they started "acting strange" shortly after their exposure to the doll.

UNEXPLAINED ILLNESS:

- None Reported.

MANIPULATION OF OBJECTS:

- The doll itself has moved on 2 occasions (overnight) while the building was locked.
- On both occasions, Jean discovered the doll approximately ten feet away from its metal chair (its original placement) upon entry into the building in the morning.
- On both occasions, the doll was surrounded by toys from the play area.
- Jean is the only person with a key to the building, and believes that it is impossible that any of the staff could have been playing a prank.
- On the day of this phone call (3/3/18) Jean found the doll moved across the room for the second time.
- This was "the final straw" which prompted a call to the museum.

UNEXPLAINED ODORS:

- None Reported.

UNEXPLAINED SOUNDS:

- None Reported.

APPARITIONS/VISUAL ANOMALIES:

- None reported by staff.
- Children have said that they have seen a "shadow man" that they described as "a giant." It is claimed that the shadow would sometimes appear while the children would cry over the doll.

UNEXPLAINED VOICES:

- Jean states that every day, there would usually be about six children that would interact with the doll.
- The kids would "hold the doll's feet and hands while talking to it."
- Jean claimed that "it looked like the kids were hearing something that the adults could not hear."
- Staff members thought that the kids just had a wild imagination, until things got more unusual.
- The kids soon began running up to staff members "hysterically" balling their eyes out because "Jolene was calling them names, and making them sad."
- Reportedly, the doll had called multiple children "ugly, stupid, not loved, and other hurtful things."

PHYSICAL CONTACT:

- None Reported.

OTHER NOTES:

- Jean is extremely frightened by these experiences.
- She states that she is "afraid of the dark," and "afraid of ghosts."
- She also states that there was never any paranormal activity within her home or daycare until "Jolene" was introduced into the building.

DESIRED RESULT / OUTCOME:

- Jean wants the doll removed as soon as possible.
- She is not interested in trying any of our techniques to coexist with the doll.
- Jean is at the point where she does not want to go back into the building until the doll is removed.

INVESTIGATOR NOTES:

- Jean seems like a very nice woman who is unfortunately, yet understandably scared.

IMPORTANT UPDATE:

- Approximately 1 hour after we ended our phone call, Jean called back and asked if there was any way that we could remove the doll today.
- I (Cody) agreed to make the trip to Connecticut this evening (3/3/18) to remove the doll from the premises.

IN-PERSON VISIT TO LOCATION

DATE OF VISIT: Sunday - March 3, 2018
INVESTIGATORS PRESENT: Cody Ray DesBiens
LOCATION RESIDENTS PRESENT: Client (Jean), 2 other staff members

PRELIMINARY NOTES UPON START OF CALL:

- Upon arrival at the daycare facility, I noticed two vehicles in the parking lot.
- When I stepped out of my car, the client (Jean) and 2 other women (who turned out to be staff members) approached me from the vehicles.
- They stated that they will not go into the building until the doll is removed.
- Jean then pointed myself in the correct direction to find the doll.
- I then made my way into the facility to find Jolene, while Jean and the staff members waited outside.
- Jolene was sitting in the middle of a room with approximately 4 small plastic toys surrounding her.
- The doll was about twelve feet away from the metal chair that Jean had originally sat her on.

CLOSING NOTES OF IN-PERSON VISIT:

- Upon meeting Jean and her staff members, it was obvious that they all were extremely freaked out over the situation surrounding the doll.
- Jean and staff were so afraid that they refused to go into the building until the doll was removed.
- Jean also stated that if I was unable to come tonight, she would've had to "talk her husband into coming down to get the doll out."

- After Jolene was placed into my vehicle, the staff members immediately showed signs of relief.
- One staff member stated that the building felt "a lot lighter now that Jolene is gone."
- I personally did not feel any paranormal symptoms when interacting with the doll.
- A follow up call will take place in about a week to see if the children are now happy in their environment.

NOTES:

DATE OF ENTRY TO MUSEUM: Monday - March 4, 2018
- Today, I (Cody) placed Jolene within the quarantine room to observe her for the next two weeks.
- We have placed her within a similar metal chair in order to recreate a similar environment to the daycare facility.

CLIENT FOLLOW UP: Sunday - March 10, 2018 - *PHONE CALL*
- Today, I (Cody) was able to reach our client (Jean) over the telephone.
- She immediately started thanking me for taking Jolene from the facility.
- Jean stated that everything is going great with the children, and that they all seem to be in "high spirits."
- She also stated that two children asked where Jolene was hiding. They were scared that she was going to jump out and scare them.
- The staff member assured the children that Jolene was now at a new home, and would not be returning.
- The children were extremely happy to hear the news of her departure.
- We ended the call with advice to call us if anything strange started to occur again.

IMPORTANT UPDATE: Saturday - April 20, 2019
3:20 pm ET
- Today was extremely interesting and mind boggling.
- As we entered the museum, we noticed that there was a burnt out lightbulb in our "Around the World" section.

- To replace the bulb, I (Cody) used Jolene's chair to reach the ceiling.
- Satori picked up Jolene as I grabbed the chair. Satori then placed Jolene down on a nearby table.
- We both then walked over to the other side of the museum (with the chair) in order to replace the lightbulb.
- I (Cody) quickly replaced the bulb (which took about 2 minutes to complete) and then we headed back to the other side of the museum to return Jolene's chair.
- When we turned the corner, we immediately noticed that Jolene was no longer in the spot where Satori and I had placed her down.
- We both stood in silence and just stared at the empty spot where she was sitting only moments ago.
- After coming back to reality, we started frantically searching the museum for Jolene.
- A few moments later, we found Jolene sitting approximately 20 feet away in the section of the museum where we do our livestream events.
- Jolene was sitting in one of our office chairs with her legs crossed.
- This was one of the most amazing personal experiences that we have ever encountered.
- I (Cody) then got extremely excited to review our security footage to see if she was captured moving across the museum.
- To get to the spot she was in, she would have had to cross the path of 2 security cameras.
- To my disbelief, Jolene was not captured on any of the cameras (which is impossible).
- The cameras did not stop recording, or malfunction in any way, which was even more mind boggling.
- To confirm, Satori and myself were the only (living) individuals in the museum, and all doors were locked behind us upon entry.
- We can not even begin to find normal or rational explanations to any of the events that have just occurred. We are completely perplexed.
- Jolene has now been moved back to her original position, sitting in her personal metal chair.
- Jolene may have had a small acclimation period with little to no activity (that we ever noticed), and is now acting up again.

IMPORTANT UPDATE: Friday - June 28, 2019
- Today, Satori and myself found Jolene (upside down) in her metal chair upon entry into the museum.
- It is impossible for the doll to fall into this position on her own, according to physics.
- It looked as if she was taken off of the chair, and placed back on the chair completely upside down.
- Satori fixed Jolene (right side up) and told her out loud that she "is free to move around the museum" as much as she wants.

IMPORTANT UPDATE: Wednesday - July 17, 2019
- Today, Satori and myself noticed that one of Jolene's shoes is now missing off of her foot.
- We searched the entire museum, and cannot seem to locate it.
- We have no explanation as to how this happened.

IMPORTANT UPDATE: Saturday - February 19, 2022
- This evening, Satori and I had Jolene on display at an event in Connecticut.
- During our presentation, we had Jolene sitting in a metal chair displayed on top of a table.
- As soon as we were done talking, in front of everyone, Jolene slid off of her chair.
- The extremely odd part about this experience was that Jolene looked as if she had stopped herself from hitting the floor.
- It seemed that her arms had wrapped themselves around the leg bars of the chair to stop the sliding.
- At the moment this happened, everyone in the room gasped in disbelief.
- It is definitely one of the more interesting experiences because multiple people witnessed the event as it was happening.

IMPORTANT UPDATE: Saturday - July 23, 2022
- This weekend, we had a large number of objects from our museum on display at an event in Woodbridge, New Jersey.

- Multiple times throughout the day today, individuals have claimed to have either seen Jolene's arms move, or have had a "strange feeling" when near her.
- We found it interesting that a majority of the reports were grouped together within a timespan of about an hour.

IMPORTANT UPDATE: Friday - November 4, 2022
- This evening, Satori and I attended an event in Waynesboro, Pennsylvania.
- For this investigation event, we have brought a selection of items from our museum.
- While in the basement of this location, Jolene was seated on a chair.
- In front of approximately ten people, paranormal equipment began to activate while Jolene fell forward in her chair, and then completely slid off onto the floor.
- This freaked everyone out beyond comprehension.

IMPORTANT UPDATE: Saturday - May 13, 2023
- This evening, we had an event at a Mine in Ogdensburg, New Jersey.
- We have brought along eight items from our museum, including Jolene.
- Throughout the event, a few hundred people viewed the objects, and Jolene was definitely a favorite as far as "strange feelings" and "odd vibes" are concerned.
- A group of four individuals also claimed to have seen Jolene's head move.
- We tried to recreate this by purposely bumping the table, but could not replicate the movement.

IMPORTANT UPDATE: Sunday - November 5, 2023
- Today, Jolene was on display at an event in New Jersey.
- She was propped up on display in a folding chair.
- In front of about ten people, Jolene's arms swung off of her lap with no explanation.
- She remains one of the most active objects within our museum collection.

POSSESSED PLAYTHINGS:

WHEN TOYS COME TO LIFE

HAUNTED TOYS

* **Residual Innocence:** Toys symbolize innocence and imagination, making them vulnerable to energies or entities drawn to such vibrancy.

* **Charged by the Child:** A child's imagination and energy may unknowingly give an item a life of its own, manifesting unusual activity.

* **Sentimental Bond:** Children often form deep attachments to their toys, infusing them with intense love, joy, or fear.

* **Witness to Trauma:** Toys are often present during significant moments in a child's life, such as loss, or tragedy, absorbing that energy.

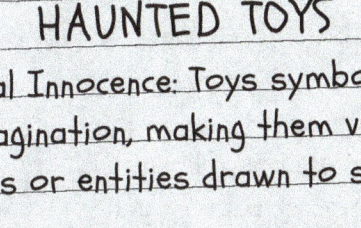

FUN FACT:
When Satori was little, she thought that her room was haunted. It turned out to be her toy "Furby" making noise.

Toys are meant to be symbols of innocence, joy, and imagination. They occupy a unique place within the stages of our lives, linking the wonder of childhood with the bittersweet, cherished memories of growing up. Yet, for some, these seemingly harmless items can take on a far more ominous role, sometimes becoming vessels for both fear and the unexplainable. Across multiple cultures and generations, stories of haunted toys have emerged—dolls that move on their own, stuffed animals that whisper in the dark, and figurines whose eyes seem to follow you around the room. What is it about these objects that makes them so unsettling? How can these items possibly cross the threshold into the world of strange?

The answer may lie in their proximity to human emotions. Toys are often deeply personal, filled with love, comfort, and sometimes sorrow. They are gifted in moments of celebration, held close during times of fear, and passed down through generations. In this way, they are accumulating layers upon layers of emotional energy. This emotional power may act as a beacon for lingering spirits, or otherworldly entities. A toy might become "possessed" or act as a spiritual anchor due to a tragic event tied to its previous owner, a wandering spirit seeking a vessel, or even just the lingering energy of those who adored it. Some believe that the childlike innocence associated with toys makes them especially attractive to supernatural entities, while others argue that human-like features, especially in cases of dolls and figurines, create an ideal imitation for entities seeking a connection to the physical world.

The resulting phenomena of haunted toys can be both bizarre and terrifying. Dolls that blink or smile on their own, toy cars that roll across the floor without a push, or music boxes that play their tunes randomly in the dead of night. Even more chilling are stories of toys that seem to intelligently communicate, offering cryptic words or laughter when no one else is paying close attention. These occurrences tap into our deepest fears, transforming objects of comfort and positive development into sources of upset or dread. A haunted toy is sort of an unsettling paradox—something that should evoke safety, but instead, becomes a symbol of terror, a betrayal of its intended purpose.

One of the most unsettling aspects of haunted toys is their powerful ability to blur the line between what's real and what's imagined. Many dismiss such encounters as tricks of the mind or overactive imaginations, but what happens when the evidence is truly undeniable? Stories of possessed or haunted objects have been verified by multiple witnesses, captured in chilling photographs or video, and even investigated by paranormal researchers. For those who have experienced the phenomenon firsthand, the question isn't whether it's real, but rather, why it happened.

Up next, we will delve into some of our chilling cases revolving around haunted or possessed playthings, exploring the stories behind them, and the deep fascination they hold over our imagination. From the infamous cases of haunted dolls such as "Annabelle," to lesser-known but equally terrifying accounts of ordinary toys turned extraordinary, these stories remind us that the portrayal of innocence can sometimes be nothing more than a fragile illusion. Sometimes, what seems lifeless may actually be anything but, and the most harmless-seeming objects can harbor some of the heaviest secrets.

THE FIRETRUCK

When Kristen Hughes' 7-year-old son, Kenny, spotted the plastic fire truck at a local charity yard sale, it seemed like the perfect new toy. Bright red, with buttons that light up the truck and play various siren sounds, it was the sort of item that could keep a child entertained for hours. Its wheels rolled smoothly, and the detailing—complete with a miniature ladder and decals, made it seem almost too good to be true for just four dollars. To Kristen, it was a simple and affordable purchase. To Kenny, however, it quickly became his new favorite belonging. She hadn't seen him so instantly attached to anything before.

At first, everything seemed completely normal. Kenny spent hours playing with his new truck, racing it across the living room floor, and pretending to save the day. Kristen would smile as she watched him in his imaginary world, grateful for the moments of peace that the toy brought into their busy home. But as time went on, Kristen began noticing something unusual. Kenny wasn't just playing, he was talking. Not to her, not to himself, but to someone else—or something else. She assumed it was harmless, just the product of an active imagination, until the conversations grew unsettling.

It began with small murmurs she couldn't quite make out, short phrases Kenny would say softly as though he were speaking to an imaginary friend. When she asked who he was talking to, he answered "The sick boy." Kristen assumed it was a new fictional friend, perhaps inspired by a show or story Kenny had recently been exposed to. But the details became specific—too specific. Kenny described the boy as having no hair, super pale skin, and a "button" on his chest. He also spoke about the boy's oversized "dress."

Kristen was unsettled, but she tried to rationalize it. Children were known to say strange things, after all, and Kenny had always been imaginative. But the unease only grew. The fire truck, which had no remote control features, began lighting up and moving on its own. At first, Kristen thought it might be a malfunction with the buttons, but the patterns didn't make sense. The siren would wail in the dead of night, and the wheels of the truck would spin suddenly when no one was near it.

Then there were the noises. Kristen and Kenny both began hearing strange, untraceable sounds: the faint roll of wheels across the floor, footsteps, and soft whistling that seemed to come from nowhere. Each sound sent shivers down Kristen's spine, but she continued to brush it off, until Kenny's sightings of "the sick boy" grew.

Kenny would tell his mom when he had seen the boy, and it was quite often. He described the young boy standing near his toy truck, watching him quietly with a sad expression. The boy's presence was so vivid to Kenny that he would instinctively pass the toy truck to him, expecting the child to take it.

The more her son interacted with the fire truck, the more frequent and intense these experiences became. Kristen noticed changes in Kennys behavior. He seemed quieter, and more withdrawn. Kristen was heartbroken, but also deeply afraid. She didn't know how to help her son, and every time she tried to take the fire truck away, Kenny protested. He would do this by saying that the boy "needed it."

By the time Kristen reached out to the museum, she was desperate for answers. In her email, she described the growing unease in her home, and how she felt as if she was being watched. She was terrified, and wanted to protect herself, and her son from whatever forces may be involved.

What had Kristen brought into her home? Was the fire truck more than just a child's toy? As we went further into this case, the story took a profoundly emotional turn. Kristen and Kenny's experience with the fire truck became a journey into the unknown. It challenged everything Kristen thought she understood about the unseen world, and the possibility of souls lingering beyond death. For her, solving the mystery was not just about restoring peace to her home but also about finding meaning in what had occurred. The fire truck was no longer just a fun find at a yard sale, it was the key to a story that had yet to be fully unlocked.

This is Case #061021, The Firetruck—a story serving as a reminder that the ordinary toys we cross paths with may carry more than just memories. For Kristen and Kenny, finding help with a haunted toy meant confronting a spirit's need for recognition.

CASE FILE

NAME: THE FIRETRUCK

CASE#: 061021

DATE: June 10, 2021

CASE #: 061021- Fire Truck

CLIENT NAME: Kristen Hughes
ALL OCCUPANTS AT LOCATION: Kristen (Client and mother), Ken (Child-7yo)
DATE OF CASE: Summer of 2021
DATE CLIENT OBTAINED OBJECT: May of 2021
CLIENT LOCATION: Norristown, Pennsylvania
LOCATION OBTAINED: Charity Yard Sale
OBJECT MANUFACTURE ORIGIN: Funrise Inc. (1992)

POINT OF CONTACT
EMAIL SENT TO PARANORMAL COUPLE ACCOUNT:
From: ***********@email.com
Date: June 10, 2021 at 8:14:28 PM EST
To: contact@paranormalcouple.com
Subject: Museum Donation

Dear Cody & Satori,
My name is Kristen Hughes and I am from Pennsylvania. I am looking to donate a toy firetruck that I recently bought at a yard sale for my son Ken. After a few days of it being home and my son playing with it, a lot of strange things have started to happen that are emotionally and mentally affecting him. If possible, please give me a call anytime after 4:00 pm weekdays or anytime on the weekend at ***-***-****.

Thank you!

PRELIMINARY PHONE INTERVIEW

PHONE INTERVIEW BY: Cody Ray DesBiens
DATE: June 13, 2021
CLIENT NAME: Kristen Hughes
PHONE NUMBER: ***-***-****
EMAIL: ***********@email.com

DESCRIPTION OF OBJECT IN QUESTION:
- Plastic red toy fire truck.
- Approximately one foot in length.
- Lights and sounds occur when buttons on the item are pushed.

HOW WAS THE OBJECT OBTAINED:
- The client (Kristen) states that the object was purchased for her son (Ken/Kenny) at a local yard sale benefiting a charity.

WHY DO YOU THINK THE OBJECT IS THE CAUSE OF THE PARANORMAL ACTIVITY:
- After bringing the toy truck home, Kristen began hearing "strange noises" in her house.
- She has witnessed Kenny having "one-way conversations" while playing with the fire truck.
- Kristen states that she has seen the truck moving, and lighting up on its own.

HOW LONG HAVE YOU BEEN AT THIS LOCATION?:
- Kristen and her son moved into their current location in October of 2019.
- She used to live in the Philadelphia area with her ex-husband (Ken's father) before their divorce.
- Kristen states that she still maintains a good relationship with her ex-husband for the sake of their child.
- It is important to note that Kenny visits with his father every other weekend.

UNEXPLAINED TEMPERATURE CHANGES:

- None Reported.

UNEXPLAINED ANOMALIES WITH ELECTRICAL DEVICES:

- The fire truck has a few buttons that make the item light up, and play multiple different noises.
- Kristen has observed the truck lighting up without any noises.
- She states that the truck is only supposed to light up when a sound is played.
- She believes that it is impossible for the lights to come on without physically pushing one of the buttons, and therefore a sound being activated.

UNEXPLAINED ILLNESS:

- None Reported.
- Kristen's son (Kenny) claims that "the boy that owns the fire truck is very sick."
- She states that Kenny has said this on multiple occasions, to the point where it makes him sad and "upset for the little boy."

MANIPULATION OF OBJECTS:

- Kristen claims that the toy fire truck has moved on its own (multiple times) with no explanation. This has occurred when Kenny would begin to play with the toy.
- One night, Kristen walked by the living room and noticed that the lights on the firetruck were on by themselves. She then witnessed the truck roll forward approximately 3 feet away from where Kenny was sitting.
- This really freaked her out because "the truck is not a remote controlled toy that moves on its own."

UNEXPLAINED ODORS:

- None Reported.

UNEXPLAINED SOUNDS:

- Kristen has also reported hearing "something that sounds like squeaky wheels rolling on the hardwood floor."
- She and her son have also heard footsteps on multiple occasions.
- When Kenny hears them, he states that "it's the sick boy walking."
- Kristen and her son have also heard an unexplained whistling sound that she can't explain, or find the source to.

UNEXPLAINED VOICES:

- Client states that she has heard the voice of a child on one occasion while she and Kenny were in the home's designated playroom together. She could not make out what was being said, but claims that it sounded like it was coming from the next room over.
- She searched the entire house, and found no one.
- Kristen states that she also looked outside to see if there were any children walking by her home, but found that "the sidewalks were empty."

APPARITIONS/VISUAL ANOMALIES:

- Kenny has seen what is believed to be the spirit of a young boy on multiple occasions.
- This phenomenon started to occur after the fire truck was brought into the home.
- Kristen thought that this was an imaginary friend until her son started saying certain words, and describing things that he shouldn't know.
- Ken has stated that "the boy is sick" and "has no hair."
- He has also expressed that the boy is not always with the truck, but "visits sometimes."
- Kenny also states that the boy is wearing something that resembles a dress. He states that it is "too big" for him.

PHYSICAL CONTACT:

- Kristen states that she believes to have felt a tug on the bottom of her shirt and pant leg on one or two occasions.

OTHER NOTES:

- Ken is being emotionally and mentally affected (on a worrisome level to Kristen) by the conversations that he is having with the boy.
- Kristen states that Kenny has started to "break down in tears sometimes" because he feels bad for the boy.
- She is very worried for her son's well being, but doesn't want to hurt the spirit's feelings.
- She states that she herself is now oftentimes afraid to stay in the home alone.

DESIRED RESULT / OUTCOME:

- Kristen is very worried about her son's emotional state.
- She wants the fire truck to go to a "good home, where the spirit of the boy will feel comfortable."
- Satori and myself have recommended that the client keep a journal of all paranormal activity until the next time we communicate.
- Because of scheduling conflicts and distance, we unfortunately will not be able to visit this home in person.
- We have scheduled a virtual video visit, interview, and location walk through with the client, and her son on June 26th, 2021 at 6:00pm ET.

INVESTIGATOR NOTES:

- We theorize that the oversized "dress" that the spirit of the boy is wearing could be a hospital gown. This would make sense if the child was sick in life.
- Satori and myself have requested the presence of our client's son (Kenny) for the upcoming video call.
- Kristen is allowing us to ask him as many questions as we want about the case.

VIRTUAL VIDEO CALL TO LOCATION

DATE OF CALL: Saturday - June 26, 2021

INVESTIGATORS PRESENT: Cody Ray DesBiens & Satori Hawes

LOCATION RESIDENTS PRESENT: Kristen (Client) & her 7 year old son Kenny

permission has been granted by the client to interview her son about the case

PRELIMINARY NOTES UPON START OF CALL:

- Kristen has given us a virtual tour of her condominium. There is a finished basement, first floor, second floor, & no attic space.
- Home seems very clean, organized, and well taken care of.
- Kenny's toy area is also very open and organized. It would be very easy to see if something was out of place, or moved around.

PARTIAL AUDIO TRANSCRIPT:

(The following audio was transcribed from a virtual video call which took place on 6/26/21 at around 6:02pm ET. Satori, myself, the client Kristen, & her 7 year old son Ken were present. This is a partial transcription.)

CODY: Okay let's start off from the beginning, if you don't mind. Could you please go over how you got the fire truck again?

KRISTEN: Absolutely! So a local organization here in town was having their annual yard sale to benefit their charity. I usually try to go every year, because sometimes you can find some cool stuff there. I actually purchased this table that the computer is on a few years ago from there.

SATORI: Oh! That's awesome.

KRISTEN: Yes! I love repainting old furniture and stuff.

KRISTEN: So this time I took Ken to the yard sale because it was my weekend with him. And when we got there, he literally was pulling me toward this table with a bunch of toys on it. He immediately spotted the fire truck and fell in love with it. He had to have it. I have never seen him so obsessed with a toy. I didn't see anything strange about it except for the fact that he has never been interested in fire trucks or firemen.

CODY: Interesting...

KRISTEN: So I paid the 4 bucks for the toy and as soon as we got home, he was playing with it.

CODY: Do you mind showing it to us?

[CLIENT PROCEEDS TO SHOW US THE TOY, AND WHAT EACH BUTTON DOES WHEN PRESSED.]

SATORI: When was the first time that he started talking about his new "friend?"

KRISTEN: So right away, I actually noticed that it looked like he was playing with someone who wasn't there. He was acting like he had a friend from school over for a playdate, but there was only 1 person talking.

CODY: And you never noticed him doing this before the truck?

KRISTEN: No, never. I have never seen anything like this before, and it only got more creepy for me when he started saying things that he had never heard before... things that myself or his father have never spoken about.

CODY: Have you talked with his father about all this?

KRISTEN: Yes, and he has no explanation for this either. He is actually super freaked out over it all, more than I am, which says a lot because we both know that we don't talk about the stuff that he is saying...

SATORI: What are some of the things he (client's son) has been telling you?

KRISTEN: Well, the first big thing I can remember that stands out to me was one day I was in the kitchen getting dinner ready, and he runs up to me and yells:
"Mommy! The boy is sick! He is really sick!"

CLIENT: I was like, "what are you talking about?" And he said that the fire truck was the boy's fire truck, and not his, and that he was very sick...

SATORI: Do you mind if we ask your son a couple quick questions?

KRISTEN: Absolutely! No problem at all. One minute...

[CLIENT WALKS AWAY TO GET HER SON OUT OF THE PLAY ROOM.]

KEN: *Hello.*

CODY: *Hey bud!*

SATORI: Hi!

KRISTEN: These are my friends Cody & Satori. They have a few questions about your fire truck friend.

SATORI: So I hear this is your new fire truck? It's really cool!

KEN: Thank you. My friend lets me play with it.

SATORI: Who is your friend? Does he have a name?

KEN: I don't know his name, but he is sick.

[CHILD IS NOTICEABLY GETTING UPSET TALKING ABOUT THIS.]

SATORI: It's okay. We are hopefully going to try to help your friend out. How did you find out he was sick?

KEN: He told me, and he doesn't have any hair.

SATORI: Did he tell you anything else about himself?

KEN: He says he has a button right here that the doctors put the medicine in.

[CHILD POINTS TO HIS CHEST AREA]

[SATORI AND MYSELF MAKE EYE CONTACT IN POSSIBLE KNOWLEDGE OF WHAT ILLNESS.]

SATORI: Do you remember what kind of clothes your friend was wearing?

KEN: He always wears the same dress.

SATORI: He wears a dress? What color is it?

KEN: White. It's very big. And blue spots.

SATORI: Wow! That's Interesting. Is he here now?

KEN: No, he only comes sometimes.

CODY: Has he ever come over when you weren't playing with the fire truck?

KEN: No, only sometimes when I play with it.

KEN: I don't like when he is sad.

[CHILD STARTS TO CRY]

CODY: Okay, I think we are all set.

[WE SAY BYE TO KENNY, AND CLIENT WALKS HIM BACK TO THE PLAY ROOM. SHE THEN COMES BACK TO THE CALL.]

CODY: Well, that was interesting for sure. A lot of things actually make a lot of sense to me, which actually gave me chills. Being a cancer patient myself, I know exactly what he meant by "a button on the boy's chest." I am almost positive that he is talking about a port. I had one, and most cancer patients receiving treatment have one. It ironically looks like a button that is placed just under the skin. It has a tube that runs into your vein so they don't have to keep trying to put IV needles in your arm. It makes it a lot easier to receive medicine. That gives me chills that he said that.

KRISTEN: Wow... now I have the chills!

SATORI: I was going to say that the "dress" sounds a lot like a hospital gown, this all makes sense now.

CODY: I know this is a shot in the dark, but would it be possible to contact the place that was having the yard sale to see if they know where they got the fire truck from?

KRISTEN: Absolutely. I can sure try.

SATORI: As far as the fire truck goes, I know you mentioned that you are a little worried about your son's emotional state...

KRISTEN: Yes, I am actually very worried because the stuff he is hearing about the boy is affecting his everyday life. He is constantly talking about it, and it makes him upset, which is not good. He is starting to want to not play with the truck in fear that he will get sad.

CODY: I have an idea, if you're interested in a little experiment?

KRISTEN: Sure!

CODY: So, Satori and myself have dealt with cases where a certain action can sometimes trigger a paranormal event. For example, when your son plays with the fire truck, it's like calling the spirit of this boy over to him. It could be both residual and intelligent at times depending on what your son is doing with the object. This can get confusing, but I think that if your son doesn't play with the fire truck, then the boy won't show up.

KRISTEN: That is interesting. So what should I do?

CODY: Well, since he is starting to not play with it as much, I recommend that you keep the fire truck in the playroom, but put it on a shelf or something where he can't reach it. Try this for a couple weeks, and see if the sightings of the boy stop.

KRISTEN: I can absolutely try that. I think it would be interesting to see if the boy only shows up if he plays with the truck.

CODY: Perfect! Let's check back in about 2 weeks or so and in the meantime, if anything happens, make sure you jot it down in your journal with the date and time.

KRISTEN: Okay. Sounds good!

[WE ENDED THE CALL, AND THE CLIENT IS GOING TO TRY TO CONTACT THE LOCATION OF THE YARD SALE TO SEE IF THEY KNOW ANYTHING ABOUT THE BACKGROUND OF THE FIRE TRUCK. WE WILL SCHEDULE A FOLLOW UP PHONE CALL IN ABOUT TWO WEEKS TO RECEIVE AN UPDATE ON THE CASE.]

CLOSING NOTES OF VIRTUAL VISIT:
- We theorize that when Kenny plays with the truck, it acts as a trigger for paranormal activity.
- After speaking with Kristen, and reviewing her paranormal event journal, all activity reported only occurs when Kenny plays with the toy.
- We have asked Kristen to place the toy back in its usual room, but in a location where her son can't come into contact with it. We hope to see a noticeable change in activity.
- Our next follow up call is in about two weeks, on Friday July 9, 2021.

NOTES:
CLIENT FOLLOW UP: Friday - July 9, 2021 - PHONE CALL
- This evening, we were able to reach our client over the telephone.
- Kristen claims that after she moved the fire truck to a high shelf, all visits from the little boy had completely stopped.
- She has also noticed a positive change in her son's attitude and emotional state.
- Kristen also states that Kenny has no interest in playing with the fire truck anymore.

- She was unable to find a direct answer as to where the fire truck came from, however, some toys have been supposedly donated from local hospitals, daycares, and private homes.
- Even though the activity has stopped, Kristen wants to donate the fire truck to a safe environment like our museum.
- We have made shipping arrangements with the client, and will be receiving the toy (via mail service) within a week or two.

DATE OF ENTRY TO MUSEUM: Thursday - July 22, 2021
- The fire truck has arrived at the museum safely.
- We have tested all of the buttons on the toy, and each button seems to be functioning in normal working order.
- The firetruck will now begin its museum quarantine period, and then be added into the museum itself.

IMPORTANT UPDATE: Saturday - August 14, 2021
7:58pm ET
- We have made a final follow up call to our client (Kristen) to check on the situation now that the toy has been removed.
- She states that everything in the home has been great, and that her son is "pretty much back to normal."
- Kristen seems very grateful that the fire truck is at a safe location.
- There has been no activity surrounding the truck at the museum as of 8/14/21.

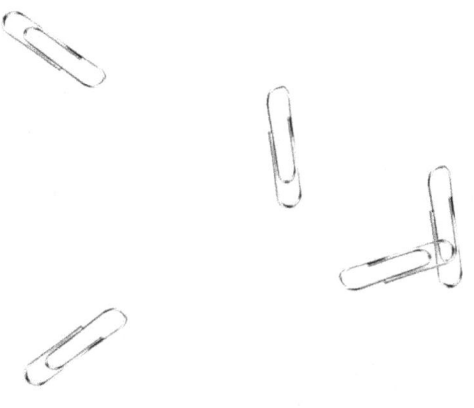

FREAKY FURBY

It was the holiday season of 1998, and Lisa Watson was among the countless number of parents scouring toy store shelves for the year's most sought after item: a "Furby." These small animatronic creatures, part furry pet, part robot, had captured the hearts of children, teens, and adults alike all across the nation. The only obstacle with this toy, however, was the inability to meet such a high demand. Lisa considered herself lucky to find one at her local toy store in Ocala, Florida, even if it wasn't the exact Furby her daughter wanted.

On Christmas morning, her daughter Lily beamed as she unwrapped the little creature with its white fur, big pink ears, and bold blinking eyes. But what began as a thoughtful gift quickly became a source of unease. By the end of that day, the Furby was acting strangely. Its voice became distorted, and its eyelids began to twitch uncontrollably. At first, Lisa dismissed the strange phenomena as a device glitch. She swapped batteries, but the unsettling behavior persisted with the same results. Then the unexplained happened, the Furby seemed to move on its own.

Lisa and her family tried to ignore it, attributing the occurrences to stress, coincidence, or faulty mechanics. But when loud noises filled the house, and sleepless nights became routine, the family made a decision. They had banished the toy to the attic, where it remained untouched for over two decades.

Now, in the midst of moving into a brand new home, Lisa found herself face-to-face with the Furby once again. Its eyes stared back at her as if it was waiting to come alive again. And soon after, the disturbances returned, cold chills, strange sensations, and that eerie, distorted voice. Determined not to let the past follow her, Lisa reached out to the museum.

What Lisa did not know was that her experiences were not the first to come under suspicion. Stories of "possessed" Furbies had circulated for years. The internet is flooded with tales of haunting voices, unexplained movements, and other strange phenomena. Could there be something more sinister at play than mere malfunctioning electronics?

As we began our investigation, we uncovered not just Lisa's story, but a strange history surrounding these once beloved toys. What started as a simple holiday gift was now a paranormal case file, one that would challenge the boundaries between nostalgia, the supernatural, and the world of the unknown.

This is Case #020322, The Freaky Furby—the moment when a child's toy became something far more unsettling.

CASE FILE

NAME: FREAKY FURBY

CASE#: 020322

DATE: February 3, 2022

CLIENT NAME: Lisa Watson
ALL OCCUPANTS AT LOCATION: Lisa (Client), Steve (Husband), Lily (Daughter that often visits home)
DATE OF CASE: February of 2022
DATE CLIENT OBTAINED OBJECT: November or December of 1998
CLIENT LOCATION: Ocala, Florida
LOCATION OBTAINED: Toy Store
OBJECT MANUFACTURE ORIGIN: Tiger Electronics - United States

POINT OF CONTACT

EMAIL SENT TO PARANORMAL COUPLE ACCOUNT:
From: **********@email.com
Date: February 3, 2022 at 5:05:52 PM EST
To: contact@paranormalcouple.com
Subject: Please Help

I have an old furby toy that I would like to give / donate to you. I am in the middle of moving to a new home and would like to get this donated before we move in if possible. How do I go about donating this? Do you come and pick it up, or do I send it somewhere? We are located in Ocala Florida. Thank you.

Lisa Watson

EMAIL REPLY:
From: contact@paranormalcouple.com
Date: February 3, 2022 at 7:22:01 PM EST
To: **********@email.com
Subject: RE: Please Help

Hi Lisa!
First off, thank you so much for reaching out to us. We are here to help!
First, we would love to know more about your story so we can come up
with the best way to assist with your situation. Every story is different
and depending on the paranormal claims surrounding an object, there
are different ways to approach the situation to have the best possible
outcome for the client.
Feel free to give us a call at your convenience so we can learn a little
more about what's happening. Please leave a message and we will call
you back. Thanks and talk soon!

Cody & Satori
--****

PRELIMINARY PHONE INTERVIEW
PHONE INTERVIEW BY: Cody Ray DesBiens & Satori Hawes
DATE: February 5, 2022
CLIENT NAME: Lisa Watson
PHONE NUMBER: ***-***-****
EMAIL: **********@email.com

DESCRIPTION OF OBJECT IN QUESTION:
- Vintage "Furby" toy.
- Operates on batteries.
- White fur, yellow beak, and pink ears.
- Approximately six inches in height.

HOW WAS THE OBJECT OBTAINED:

- The client (Lisa) explains that during the holiday season of 1998, the "Furby" toys were the most popular items to get your hands on.
- Apparently, people were camping out in front of toy stores just to try and get their hands on one.
- Luckily for Lisa, she states that she was able to purchase one at a local toy store in Ocala. This store is now closed.
- She expresses that she had been trying to purchase one for her daughter (Lily) at the time (who is now 32 today) because it was the main toy that she was asking for on her Christmas list that year.
- Lisa recalls that it wasn't the "ideal color" that her daughter was looking for, but at that point in time it didn't matter. As long as she had one to give her daughter for Christmas, Lisa was happy.

WHY DO YOU THINK THE OBJECT IS THE CAUSE OF THE PARANORMAL ACTIVITY:

- Immediately after Lisa's daughter (Lily) opened her Christmas gifts for the holiday of 1998, she wanted to play with her new Furby toy right away.
- Lisa took it out of the box, and installed batteries.
- A few moments later, Lisa was alone in Lily's room with the toy, and placed it on top of the dresser.
- The client states that this is when things began to get a bit strange.
- A day or two after the activity began, and her daughter also becoming aware and uneasy, Lisa placed the Furby in a box. She then had her husband (Steve) bring the box up into the attic.
- She states that nothing paranormal has ever occurred, or has been experienced up until this point.
- Fast forward to a few days ago (about 24 years later), while moving boxes, Lisa found the old Furby. After this, a lot of the old paranormal experiences began to occur again.
- This prompted Lisa to contact the museum.

UNEXPLAINED ODORS:

- None to report.

HOW LONG HAVE YOU BEEN AT THIS LOCATION?:

- The client (Lisa) and her husband (Steve) have lived in their home for about 25 years.
- They have recently sold the home, and are currently moving / downsizing to a smaller house.

UNEXPLAINED TEMPERATURE CHANGES:

- Lisa states that she hasn't experienced temperature changes, but has experienced "quick cold chills." This has begun to happen quite often over the past few days.
- She states that "it also sometimes feels like a static charge, when all the hairs on your arms stand up."

UNEXPLAINED ANOMALIES WITH ELECTRICAL DEVICES:

- The Furby itself did some unsettling things when it was first turned on, back in 1998.
- Lisa states that it soon began talking in this "creepy raspy voice," but you couldn't make out what was being said.
- She states that it sounded "very dark and demonic," to the point that her daughter also got scared.
- The eyelids also began blinking uncontrollably, which was extremely odd.
- At first, Lisa assumed that it was either a bad battery, or the item actually malfunctioning.
- After replacing the batteries with no positive changes, what happened next made her more unsettled. The activity surrounding this item convinced her that "it wasn't a normal explanation."

UNEXPLAINED ILLNESS:

- One thing that Lisa remembers from 1998, was that everyone in the house could not get any sleep while the Furby was in Lily's room.
- She states that "it sounds crazy," and then continued describing how it got to the point where it felt like the toy was keeping them awake on purpose.
- After putting the toy in the attic, this phase soon passed.

- She wasn't sure if this was caused by something natural such as stress and anxiety, or if it was paranormal.
- Either way, it eventually went back to normal, and the family didn't worry about it much.

MANIPULATION OF OBJECTS:
- This was the first time that Lisa was absolutely freaked out.
- After she had originally placed the toy on the dresser (back in 1998), she turned around and walked out of her daughter's room.
- As she was walking down the hall, she heard the "creepy demonic voice" again, and decided to turn around to check on the toy.
- When she turned the corner back into the room, she screamed.
- The Furby was now on the floor, standing upright. This was seemingly impossible for the toy to do on its own.
- She also confirmed that Lily was nowhere near her room when the event occurred back in 1998, and Lily had no idea that it had even happened until only recently.

UNEXPLAINED SOUNDS:
- Lisa states that they have heard "weird loud bangs in the house" over the years. They could never find a source or reason for the sounds, but they are not sure if it is at all paranormal or not.

UNEXPLAINED VOICES:
- Besides the Furby talking incoherently on its own, there were a few other instances in which Lisa and Steve believe that they had heard a creepy voice coming from the attic.
- The even stranger fact is that when Lisa placed the Furby in the box (in preparation for the attic back in 1998), she took the batteries out to prevent corrosion.
- As usual, they couldn't understand or make out any words that were being said, but they were completely sure that it was the Furby.
- Since finding the Furby again recently, they have not heard the voice, or installed new batteries.

APPARITIONS/VISUAL ANOMALIES:

- None Reported.

PHYSICAL CONTACT:

- None Reported.

DESIRED RESULT / OUTCOME:

- Lisa does not want to bring the toy to their new home.
- If there is something paranormal attached to the Furby, Lisa does not want it to follow her to their new place.
- Lisa is ready to ship the item as soon as possible.

INVESTIGATOR NOTES:

- Due to the fact that the toy was purchased "new," we find it unlikely that the Furby had an attachment, or an energy following it back in 1998.
- With that being said, some of the other claims are intriguing, but confusing to us at the same time.
- It may be difficult to figure out what, or who has been interacting with this family, and why.
- We believe that it could be two completely separate events happening at the same time.
- For example, the Furby could normally be malfunctioning, and a spirit could be causing the other claims in their home.
- Either way, Lisa wants to ship the toy out as soon as possible. We have given her instructions on how to remove the item correctly from the home, while also setting her intentions.

NOTES:

IMPORTANT UPDATE: Sunday - February 6, 2022

- After a quick internet search, there have been thousands of reports regarding individuals having creepy and unnerving experiences with their Furby's throughout the years. Many of these individuals believe that their Furby was / is possessed.

- We also found many reports of other Furby's talking in creepy voices ranging from deep, raspy, slow motion, and even other unprogrammed languages.
- Another interesting fact is that in the 1990's, there were published reports stating that The National Security Agency (NSA) believed that Furby's could be used by foreign spies. They believed that these toys posed a national security threat. The NSA went as far as banning Furby's from their office buildings in case they could listen in on classified conversations, and relay that secret information.

DATE OF ENTRY TO MUSEUM: Tuesday - February 15, 2022
- Today, Satori and I received the Furby in the mail.
- We first placed new batteries in the toy to test it out, and nothing happened. We could not get the Furby to move at all.
- We then placed the Furby on a small table within the quarantine room to watch over it for the next two weeks.

CLIENT FOLLOW UP: Friday - March 4, 2022 - PHONE CALL
- Satori & myself were able to reach our client (Lisa) over the phone.
- She explained that they have officially moved into their new home, and "feel great."
- We filled Lisa in on the fact that she was not alone in her Furby experiences, and that her case was one of thousands of reported problematic Furbys.
- She expressed her appreciation for our help, and stated that nothing unusual has happened in their new home as of yet. She states that she will contact us as soon as possible if something does happen.

IMPORTANT UPDATE: Friday - May 27, 2022

- Today, we entered the museum to prepare for an upcoming event this weekend.
- While collecting some of our items for the event, we noticed that the Furby was turned around. The back of the toy was now facing forward on the shelf.
- We, of course, have no logical explanation as to how or why that happened.
- Because the item is still a rather new addition to our museum, we do believe that it could have possibly been another energy (from another item within our collection) interacting with the toy.
- We fixed the Furby, and left the museum.

IMPORTANT UPDATE: Saturday - June 11, 2022

- Today, Satori & I had noticed that the Furby was, once again, spun completely around.
- We are now (definitely) under the impression that another spirit or energy is not fond of the Furby.
- We had a similar interaction happen a few years ago with another object (doll) in our possession named "Liza."
- On a few occasions, we would enter the museum and find other dolls (within Liza's vicinity) spun around completely. Some dolls just had their heads turned around, facing away from "Liza."
- The similar interaction with the dolls only began to occur when "Liza" was incorporated into the museum, and the designated "Doll" section. Liza has since been moved out of that section, and activity revolving around spinning dolls has stopped.
- We believe this case (with the new Furby) to be a similar interaction, so we have moved the Furby to a different part of the museum.

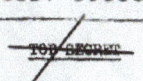

~~TOP SECRET~~

~~TOP SECRET~~

SUBJECT: Christmas Toys with Artificial Intelligence
DATE: 9 Dec 1998 14:31:00   -0500
CLASSIFICATION: CLASSIFIED
SECURITY CONTROL MARKING: FOR OFFICIAL USE ONLY

It has come to my attention that a new toy on the
market called a "Furby" has an Artificial
Intelligent chip on-board. An office I recently
visited had two of these in their spaces.
Apparently these stuffed critters learn from
nearby speech patterns.
It would seem to me that this would be a security
issue in that they can pick up any spoken language
and repeat it.
This will need to be addressed as soon as possible.

SPY AGENCY BANS FURBYS
NSA says "Not allowed for security reasons"

Washington, D.C. - The National Security Agency (NSA) has officially banned Furbys, the once-popular robotic toy, from its premises due to fears they could pose a security threat. The agency announced its decision this week, citing concerns that the interactive toys, which can record and mimic speech, might inadvertently capture and leak classified conversations.

"While Furbys were designed as harmless children's toys, their built-in microphones and ability to 'learn' speech present a potential risk in sensitive environments," said an NSA spokesperson.

The decision dates back to a 1999 rumor that Furbys were secretly recording devices, though this has been debunked by their manufacturer, Tiger Electronics. Despite this, experts warn that even simple technology can be exploited in high-security areas.

Employees have been instructed to leave the nostalgic toys at home, and visitors bringing Furbys to NSA facilities may face confiscation. While the toys are no longer widely produced, this decision serves as a reminder of the growing intersection of technology and security concerns.

This latest move highlights the agency's commitment to safeguarding national secrets—one talking toy at a time.

SISTER BELLE

Memories of childhood are often able to bring us comfort, a retreat to simpler times. For Jen Brooks, however, one memory refused to fade into the past, haunting her for more than fifty years. It was tied to a birthday gift that she was given back in 1970, a seemingly innocent doll by the name of "Sister Belle." Jen had been no more than eight years old when she first unwrapped the toy. Its large cartoon-like head, cloth body, and cheerful pull-string voice were meant to bring a rush of both joy and warmth, but instead, Sister Belle became a source of unexplainable terror that would echo throughout the decades.

At first, Jen adored the doll. She began carrying it everywhere like a constant companion. It wasn't long before strange activity began to occur. Late at night, Jen and her younger sister would begin to hear the doll's voice breaking the silence of their home. Its programmed phrases rang out eerily in the darkness. Sometimes, the girls would hear Sister Belle laugh, or even scream, a sound that the doll wasn't programmed to make. One night, the doll even began to cry. This was not a sound from any pull-string mechanism, it was something human-like and entirely unnatural. The sisters' terror was worsened by their parents' dismissive attitudes, which offered no support.

The doll's disturbing presence truly peaked in its mysterious disappearance. One day, the toy simply vanished without a trace. The young girls never saw it again, at least not until much later. Its vanishing did not end the paranormal strangeness within their lives. Radios would turn on and scan frequencies, even when unplugged. Whispers and footsteps could be heard in distant rooms. The home, once a symbol of safety, became a place of unease. Jen and her sister never spoke of Sister Belle again. As the years passed, Jen eventually left her childhood home behind.

Decades later, in early 2023, Jen was thrown back into the pit of those memories. After her mother's passing, she and her husband (Cory) returned to her family home in Cedar Rapids, Iowa, to prepare it for sale. Contractors began the renovations in order to remodel and modernize the space, starting with knocking down walls to open the layout. When the first wall came down, the workers approached Jen with a strange expression. They had found something they weren't expecting.

It was Sister Belle.

The doll was pristine, as if it had been placed in the wall only moments ago. Jen found herself unable to breathe as she held it in her hands, the same doll that had mysteriously vanished more than fifty years ago. How had it ended up there? This question plagued her as she made the decision to take Sister Belle back to her own home.

Bringing the doll back invited not only memories, but also something far more disturbing. From the moment Sister Belle entered the house, Jen felt uneasy. Nights soon became sleepless, her thoughts now being consumed by the doll's presence. She began to hear faint noises that resembled distant laughing, and a child's voice. One night, Jen awoke to find the doll lying on the floor, even though she was certain that it had been left on a high shelf. A cold breeze swept through the room as she picked it up, sending deep chills throughout her body.

Cory, her husband, had always been a skeptic. Ghosts and curses were the stuff of fiction novels and movies to him. He had never experienced anything remotely close to paranormal activity. Sister Belle, however, quickly changed that. One evening, as Cory sat in his recliner, he heard a knock at the door. After leaving the comfort of his chair to answer it, he strangely found that there was no one outside. Turning back toward the living room, he stopped dead in his tracks. Cory was left shocked by what he had seen, and remained quiet for the rest of the night.

The couple's dogs, normally calm and affectionate, also began barking at empty corners, and refused to enter certain rooms. Electronics flickered on and off unpredictably, and Jen's growing attachment to the doll constantly battled with her instinctive fear of it. The final straw came when Jen heard a giggle in the early morning hours, followed by a loud bang. While investigating the noise, she found Sister Belle lying face down in the hallway. This activity was enough to send Jen searching for help.

In March of that year, Jen emailed us, asking how to properly dispose of a haunted or cursed object. She didn't want to anger whatever might be attached to the doll, but knew that she couldn't live with it anymore.

After weeks of sleepless nights, Jen finally packed up Sister Belle and sent it away. In follow up conversations, she admitted that part of her still felt attached to the doll. It was sort of a surviving symbol of her childhood, but she also knew that she could never allow it to stay in her home, and life any longer.

Sister Belle now resides safely within the museum. What had caused the doll to move, speak, and show emotions? Why did the possible spirit presence linger, even after multiple decades? These questions remain a haunting reminder of how the past can oftentimes refuse to stay buried.

This is Case #031123, Sister Belle. A chilling example of how an innocent childhood item can become a lifelong source of fear. For Jen Brooks, it is a story of perseverance, mystery, and the power of the unknown to reach across time, leaving its mark in ways that defy all explanation.

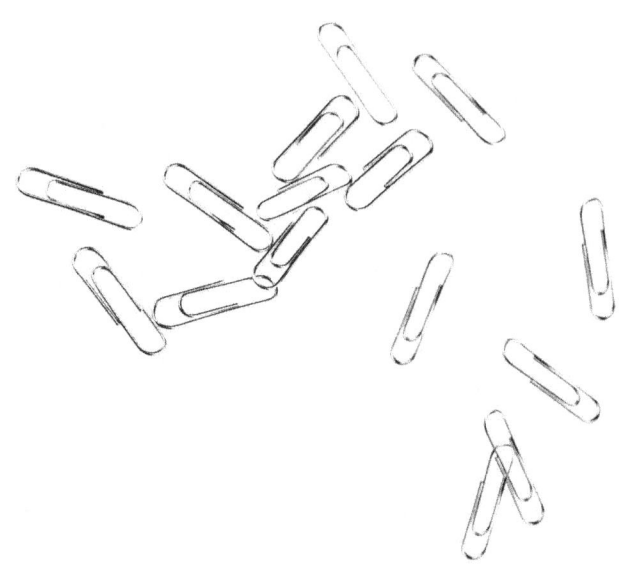

NAME: SISTER BELLE

CASE#: 031123

DATE: March 11, 2023

CASE #: 031123 - Sister Belle

CLIENT NAME: Jen Brooks
ALL OCCUPANTS AT LOCATION: Jen (Client), Cory (Husband), Two Dogs
DATE OF CASE: From approximately 1970, to March of 2023
DATE CLIENT OBTAINED OBJECT: Around June of 1970
CLIENT LOCATION: Cedar Rapids, Iowa
LOCATION OBTAINED: Birthday Gift
OBJECT MANUFACTURE ORIGIN: Mattel - USA (1960's)

POINT OF CONTACT
EMAIL SENT TO PARANORMAL COUPLE ACCOUNT:
From: *********@email.com
Date: March 11, 2023 at 9:53:28 PM EST
To: contact@paranormalcouple.com
Subject: HAUNTED OBJECT

Hello
Is there a way to properly dispose of haunted / cursed objects? I have seen many television shows and movies on the subject and I would hate to do something wrong. Any advice would be greatly appreciated. We are sort of freaked out at the moment and just want to do the right things to not make it worse for us.
Thank you!

PRELIMINARY PHONE INTERVIEW

PHONE INTERVIEW BY: Cody Ray DesBiens & Satori Hawes
DATE: Tuesday - March 14, 2023
CLIENT NAME: Jen Brooks
PHONE NUMBER: ***-***-****
EMAIL: *********@email.com

DESCRIPTION OF OBJECT IN QUESTION:

- Vintage doll, approximately 16 inches in length.
- Plastic head and a stuffed cloth body.
- Pull string located on the neck that activates about four to six different phrases.

HOW WAS THE OBJECT OBTAINED:

- The client (Jen) was given this doll as a birthday gift when she was around eight to ten years old.
- She states that this would have been somewhere around the year 1970.
- She was given the doll in her parents' home at the time. They have now both passed on.
- Since the passing of her mother last year, they have decided to sell her parent's old home.
- The object went missing a few months after receiving it back in the 70's.

WHY DO YOU THINK THE OBJECT IS THE CAUSE OF THE PARANORMAL ACTIVITY:

- Once receiving the object, Jen remembers playing with it immediately.
- She states that she fell in love with it, until strange things began to occur.
- She and her younger sister clearly remember seeing the doll move by itself in a rocking chair one evening.
- She states that their parents tried to convince them that the doll just fell, but the kids did not believe that at all.
- About a week later, the doll mysteriously went missing.
- This was the start of a series of strange events.

HOW LONG HAVE YOU BEEN AT THIS LOCATION?:

- Jen's parents purchased the home in the late 1940's.
- She states that they had never witnessed anything strange in that home before, besides the doll.
- Today, Jen and her husband (Cory) have been in their home for close to twenty years now, and they (including their kids) have never experienced anything strange.

UNEXPLAINED ILLNESS:

- None Reported.

UNEXPLAINED ODORS:

- None Reported.

UNEXPLAINED SOUNDS:

- The creepiest part of this story is what would happen at night.
- It became a weekly occurrence that in the middle of the night, Jen and her sister would hear the doll talking somewhere in the house.
- Sometimes they would even hear it laughing, or screaming.
- This scared the girls severely, especially because you have to manually pull the string for the doll to even talk.
- The sounds eventually stopped, a couple months later, for approximately three years.
- One night while laying in bed, the girls remember talking to each other when, all of a sudden, they began to hear the doll crying.
- It was not a sound that the doll was programmed to make. It really startled them.
- After that night, they never heard the doll again.

UNEXPLAINED ANOMALIES WITH ELECTRICAL DEVICES:

- One evening, around the time that the doll had gone missing back in the 1970's, Jen and her sister experienced their radio turn on and scan for about five seconds without being plugged in.
- She states that it was so loud that their mom had heard it scan as well.

MANIPULATION OF OBJECTS:

- After Jen's mom passed away, she and Cory decided to sell the home.
- Before listing the house on the market, the realtor suggested that they make some renovations to make the home more appealing to possible buyers.
- They immediately hired contractors to do the work.
- The first project was knocking down two walls to make the floor plan a little more open.
- Upon knocking down the first wall in the living room, the contractors approached Jen and Cory and stated that they had found something.
- It was the doll.
- Jen has no reasonable explanation as to how the doll ended up in the wall. "It just doesn't make sense."

UNEXPLAINED VOICES:

- After finding the doll recently, she didn't have the heart to throw it away.
- She took it from the contractors, and brought it home to her house.
- That night she could not fall asleep. Memories of the past flooded her head, and she just felt like "something was off."
- In the early morning hours she had heard a bang, and then a giggle.
- She got up to investigate, and found that the doll was on the floor.

UNEXPLAINED TEMPERATURE CHANGES:

- Jen states that the only time a temperature change occurred is when the doll was being relocated to her current home.
- On the car ride there, a cold breeze swept through the vehicle.
- She expresses that it was extremely "odd and unnerving."

APPARITIONS/VISUAL ANOMALIES:

- It is important to note that Jen's husband (Cory) has never had a paranormal experience. He also has never really believed much in ghosts.
- On the evening that the doll was brought home, Cory states that he had heard a knock at the door.

- He then got up from his recliner, opened the door, and found no one there.
- When he turned around to go back to his chair, he claims to have seen a "white cloud blob move across the room" about ten feet away from him.
- He states that he had never seen anything like this in his lifetime, and that this experience made him more of a believer in the afterlife.

PHYSICAL CONTACT:
- None Reported.

DESIRED RESULT / OUTCOME:
- Jen wants to "dispose" of the doll properly.
- She states that she has not gotten a good night's sleep since the doll has been brought into her current home.
- We have instructed Jen to place the doll in their tool shed (on the property) until she is able to go to the post office, and ship the item.

INVESTIGATOR NOTES:
- We are not sure what could possibly be attached to this doll. Jen believes that it was "regifted" when she originally received it.
- She is not sure where her parents got the item from. She states that her family did not have a lot of money growing up, and a lot of their gifts were "used or secondhand."
- No matter what, or who is with the doll, we believe that removing the item from her living space will fix her paranormal situation.

NOTES:
DATE OF ENTRY TO MUSEUM: Saturday - March 25, 2023
- Today, Satori and I received the doll in the mail.
- We tested the doll by pulling its string a few times and it seems to be in good condition. It is in good working order for its age.
- We have also placed the doll on a stand in the quarantine room for further observation.

IMPORTANT UPDATE: Sunday - March 26, 2023

- After doing some research, we have found that the name of this doll is in fact "Sister Belle."
- This toy was released by the company "Mattel" in 1961.
- This means that by the time the client received the doll, it was approximately the same age as her.

CLIENT FOLLOW UP: Saturday - April 8, 2023 - PHONE CALL

- Today, Satori and I were able to speak with our client (Jen) on the phone.
- She states that she is finally getting sleep, and feels well rested again now that the doll is out of her house.
- She states that part of her still feels attached to the doll, and even misses it.
- We expressed that all she has to do is contact us if she ever wants it back.
- She immediately responded with two words... "No thanks."

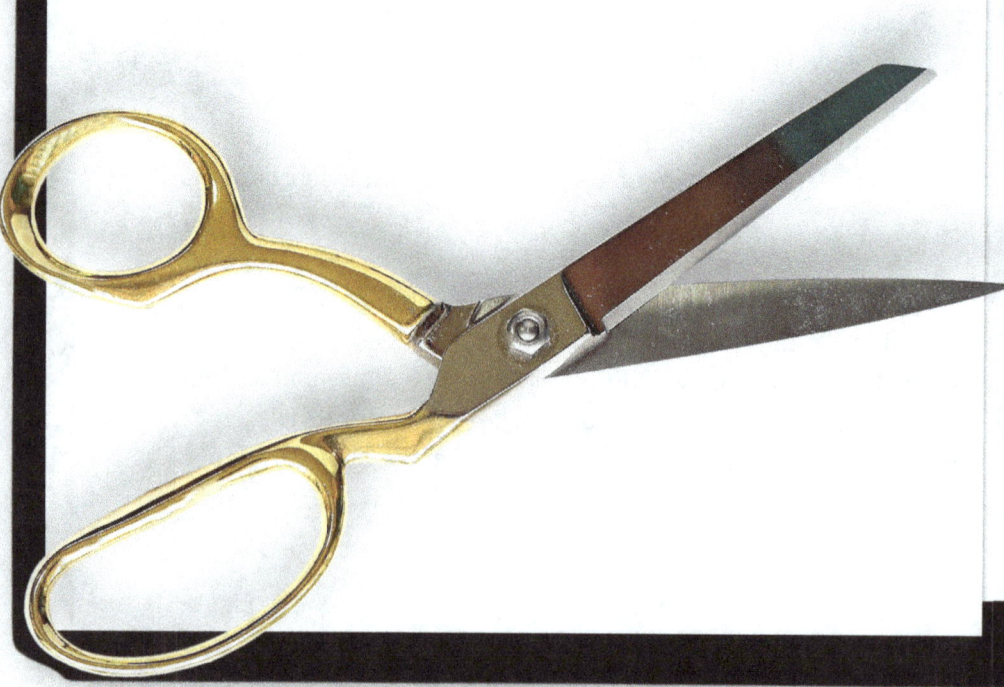

Famous talking Pa

K SISTER BELLE. From "Matty's Funday Funnies" TV show. Bright yellow yarn hair, striped pinafore. Soft, cuddly body, sturdy plastic head. 16" high.
96 B 0412H—Wt. 2 lbs. 8 oz.. **7.78**

"I love you, too."

SISTER BELLE says "I love you"... or any of ten other phrases when you pull a little ring. She is just one of the creative, imaginative products made by Mattel Toymakers. If your child should see a Mattel toy on one of our television programs, and ask for that toy, you can be confident of thoughtful originality and unfailing quality. That quality is important to children... and to us. Because ours is a most rewarding business. We make children happy.

50% Savings
TALKING MATTY MATTEL AND SISTER BELLE
YOUR CHOICE $3⁸³

I Love You

I'm Matty Mattel

10 Sister Belle, the lovable talking rag doll, 17 in. tall. Pull the ring, she says "I love you; Sing me a song," and others. With pinafore, yarn hair.
48 T 3872—Ship. wt. 2 lbs. 9 oz.....Was $7.67. Now $3.83

11 Matty the Talking Boy wears T-shirt, shorts, shoes, has red hair, stuffed body. Says "I like you; Let's play cowboy," and others when you pull ring.
48 T 3864—Ship. wt. 2 lbs. 4 oz. 17 in. tall. Was $7.67..$3.53

Original advertisements for the "Sister Belle" Doll

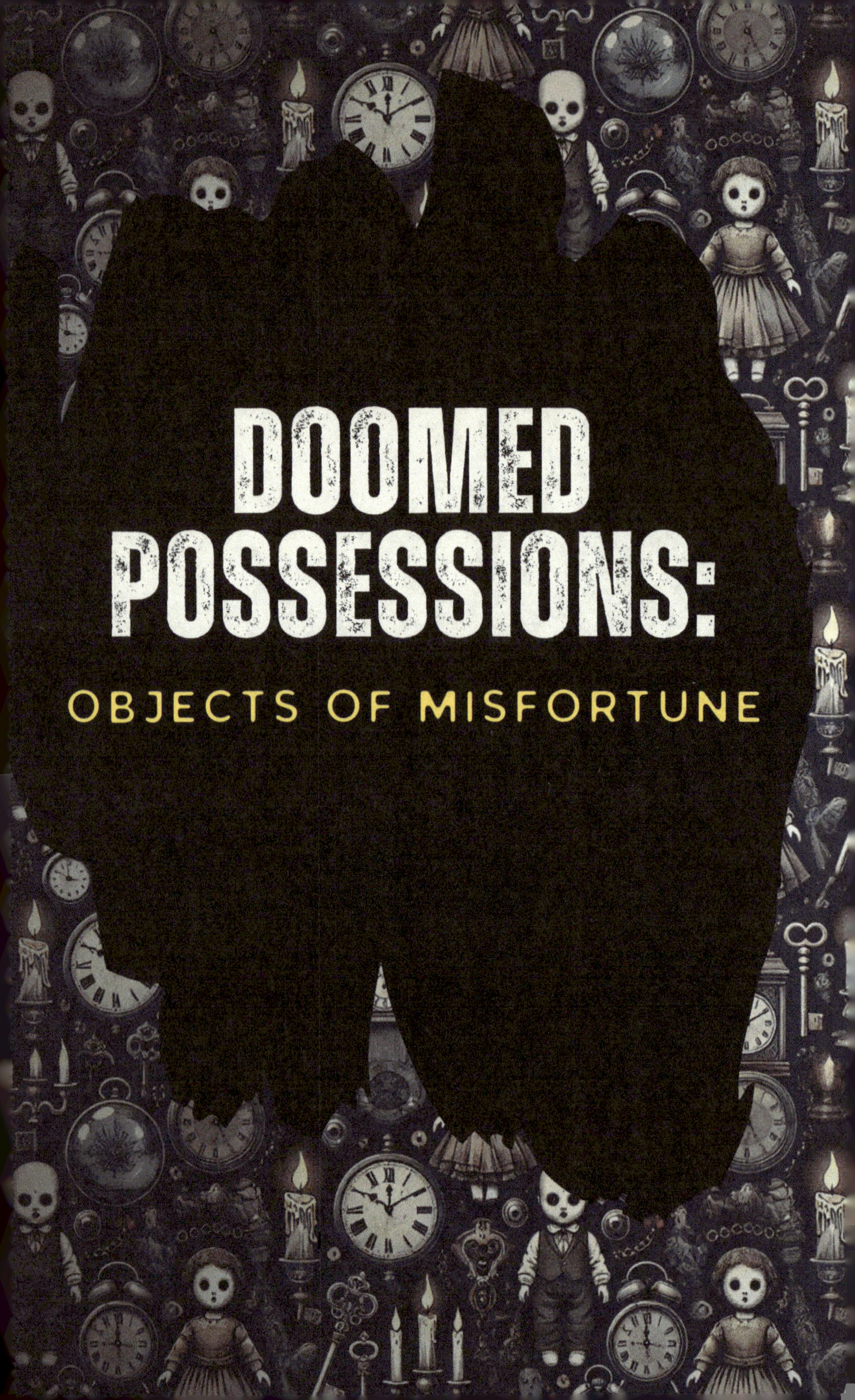

DOOMED POSSESSIONS:

OBJECTS OF MISFORTUNE

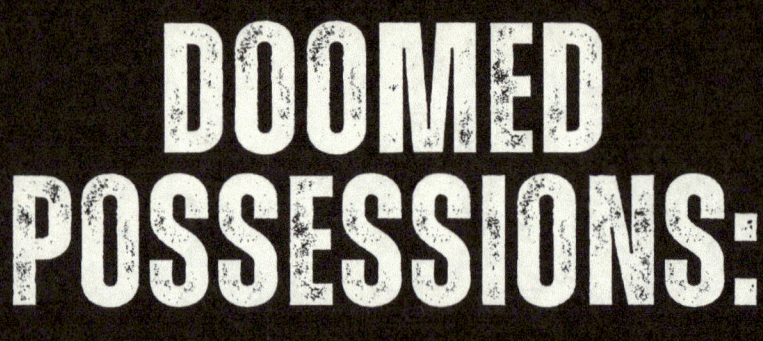

WHY WOULD IT CAUSE BAD LUCK?

* Malevolent Intent: The object could be cursed or intentionally filled with energy meant to cause harm, or bring misfortune.

* Chain of Misfortunes: A history of bad luck tied to an object perpetuates a pattern, influencing future owners psychologically, or energetically.

* Negative Energy Imprint: An object may retain harmful emotions such as anger, jealousy, or despair from its previous owner, or creator.

FUN FACT: Some of the most commonly carried lucky charms are:
- FOUR LEAF CLOVERS
- LUCKY COINS
- RELIGIOUS SYMBOLS
- CRYSTALS OR STONES
- A RABBIT'S FOOT
- PERSONAL KEEPSAKES

Throughout history, certain objects have seemingly carried with them a shadow of misfortune— a legacy filled with unexplained accidents, tragedies, and even death for those who dare to take them into possession. Tales of these possibly cursed artifacts haunt the archives of folklore, each account a bit more unsettling than the last. These items can be found anywhere from private collections, to forgotten attics, dusty museum basements, and even directly in the hands of unsuspecting buyers who find themselves drawn to a new piece. Whether they are ancient relics, family heirlooms, or unassuming trinkets from the not-so-distant past, these objects appear to radiate a sort of energy that disrupts the lives of their owners. For centuries, people have reported an eerie, relentless pattern of bad luck or misfortune linked to such items, leaving us to wonder: what could possibly cause these inanimate objects to manifest such a dark intention?

The concept of cursed objects is universal, spanning nearly every culture and continent. Oftentimes, these objects are believed to hold onto the energy and intention of their previous owners, or to absorb emotions like grief, rage, and despair that linger long after the original owner has passed away. Some paranormal theorists argue that residual energy is responsible for what many identify as a curse, that objects are acting as emotional sponges and retaining the most intense human feelings. It's thought that items connected to particularly traumatic or violent events might bear the weight of such experiences. The sorrow, pain, or rage may become imprinted on the item, influencing all who come into contact with it. This, in turn, may lead those who are exposed to the item into a cycle of misfortune.

In other cases, some theorize that curses appear to have less to do with past trauma, and more to do with an unseen force that can be attached to an object. Some believe that spirits, entities, or other supernatural forces beyond comprehension may latch onto items and, through them, find ways to influence and distress the living. These forces may use an object as a gateway, manipulating it to affect surroundings, and those nearby. Others suggest that these objects may serve as vessels for powerful curses and spells cast long ago—perhaps a curse from someone betrayed or wronged, or from a civilization whose sacred items were desecrated or stolen. This theory suggests a deeper and more intentional cause for the misfortune that these objects may bring, as if they were created or modified specifically for the purpose of bringing suffering to anyone who dared disturb them.

Up next, we will explore some of the more intriguing examples of these unlucky possessions from our collection, items that have inexplicably caused pain, sorrow, and misfortune to those who have encountered them. Are these items truly cursed? Or could there be psychological factors, hidden history, or mere coincidence at play?

One thing is certain: these stories show us that some objects, no matter how beautiful or supposedly harmless, may hold a legacy of doom that only the bravest, or most unknowing would dare to test.

THE PARANORMAL COUPLES
HAUNTED MUSEUM OF
OBJECTS, ODDITIES AND CURIOSITIES

THE OMEN DOLL

Winters in Woodstock, Vermont, carry a certain magic with them. The snowy forest, and the soft glow of antique shop windows invite people to linger. For Lorraine Cook, a longtime resident and passionate collector of dolls, these stores offer endless opportunities to discover treasures. She took pride in her collection, creating elaborate displays that shifted with the seasons and holidays.

In December of 2020, Lorraine came across a doll that seemed perfect for her wintertime collection. It had a rather realistic porcelain face with delicate features, blonde hair, and an eye-catching maroon coat. The design captured the feeling of the season, and Lorraine knew it would be the newest centerpiece of her display. She quickly purchased the doll and brought it home, eager to arrange it with her other items.

But after she left the shop, a strange unease began to settle over her, an unexpected heaviness that she hadn't felt before. She attributed it to the cold Vermont winter and tried to shake it off, but the feeling still lingered. By the time Lorraine reached her house, the unease had grown into an episode of anxiety. She had lived alone for over a decade now, her only companion being an aging tabby cat, and her home had always been a place of nothing but comfort and familiarity. Yet, with the doll now in her possession, the atmosphere completely changed.

The activity began with only subtle disturbances. The house, though well insulated, seemed significantly colder. The flickering of lights soon became a regular occurrence, mysteriously dimming or shutting off without reason. Lorraine even heard faint creaks and muffled movements at night, though she tried to dismiss them as the natural sounds of her older home.

Then Lorraine began to see her.

One morning, while driving to a doctor's appointment, Lorraine spotted a girl standing in the middle of the road. it seemed as if the girl had appeared out of thin air. Startled, Lorraine swerved to avoid hitting her, and completely lost control of the car. It veered off the road and collided with a tree. Shaken but unharmed, Lorraine looked back to where the girl had been standing, but the road was empty.

Weeks later, the girl appeared again, this time in Lorraine's living room. Moments after the sighting, Lorraine was faced with one of the most painful situations possible. She received a phone call from the hospital informing her that her father had passed away unexpectedly. The timing of the entity's appearances began to feel deliberate, as though she were an omen of tragedy.

After these terrifying encounters, Lorraine was preparing to meet a friend for an outing when the girl appeared once more. Terrified of what might happen, Lorraine canceled her plans. The decision resulted in a fractured relationship, but Lorraine was confident in her choice after her previous situations.

By February of 2021, Lorraine had reached her breaking point. The doll, once a cherished new inclusion to her collection, now felt like a lingering curse. Her home, once a place of safety and peace, had become a source of all her nerves. The spiritual presence of her late husband, which she had often felt in the house, was gone. She believed that the doll had driven him away too.

On the day that Lorraine sent the doll to our museum, she experienced one final encounter. As she was settling in for the night, the lights flickered rapidly, and the girl appeared at the foot of her bed. For the first time, the girl spoke, her voice cold and haunting. She uttered only two words before vanishing for the last time.

"The Omen Doll" now resides in our collection. Its chilling history is preserved as a strong reminder of the unseen forces that can attach themselves to even the most innocent of objects. Lorraine's experience emphasizes a profound truth: even the most beautiful and inviting things can carry hidden risks.

The question of why the doll is tied to such activity remains unanswered. Is it merely an anchor for an existing entity, or did the doll itself possess some inherent power? These are mysteries we may never solve. But one thing is clear, some objects are better left on the shelves, no matter how perfect they seem.

This is Case #020921, The Omen Doll, a chilling account of one woman's encounter with the impending.

CASE FILE

THE PARANORMAL COUPLE'S
HAUNTED MUSEUM OF
OBJECTS, ODDITIES AND CURIOSITIES

NAME: THE OMEN DOLL

CASE#: 020921

DATE: February 9, 2021

CASE #:020921 - The Omen Doll

CLIENT NAME: Lorraine Cook
ALL OCCUPANTS AT LOCATION: Lorraine (client), Cat (pet)
DATE OF CASE: End of 2020 ~ Start of 2021
DATE OBJECT OBTAINED: December 2020
CLIENT LOCATION: Woodstock, Vermont
LOCATION OBTAINED: Local Antique Store
OBJECT MANUFACTURE ORIGIN: Unknown

POINT OF CONTACT
EMAIL SENT TO PARANORMAL COUPLE ACCOUNT:
From: *************@email.com
Date: February 9, 2021 at 7:41:58 PM EST
To: WEBSITE - contact@paranormalcouple.com
Subject: I Need Help

Hi Satori and Cody,
My name is Lorraine and I am dealing with a scary situation. I am a doll collector and I like to display different pieces of my collection depending on the time of year or holiday. Last December I fell in love with a new doll at an antique store that I thought would fit great with my winter collection.
Well as soon as I walked out of the store, I got a random bad feeling and things immediately started to go wrong and it progressed as time went on. The spirit or entity with the doll is definitely the problem, that much I am sure of.
I am concerned about what to do next. I want to properly have the doll removed from my house, but I also want to be cleansed of the negative energy that this doll has brought with it. Thank you and I look forward to your response. GOD BLESS.
-Lorraine

PRELIMINARY PHONE INTERVIEW

PHONE INTERVIEW BY: Cody Ray DesBiens & Satori Hawes
DATE: Friday - February 12, 2021
CLIENT NAME: Lorraine Cook
PHONE NUMBER: ***-***-****
EMAIL: *************@email.com

DESCRIPTION OF OBJECT IN QUESTION:
- Doll with porcelain face, hands, and feet.
- Blonde hair, wearing a dress and a maroon colored coat.

HOW WAS THE OBJECT OBTAINED:
- The client (Lorraine) states that she frequently shops at a specific local antique store.
- Lorraine states that she is "always on the lookout for beautiful dolls" to add to her extensive collection.
- This doll in particular was purchased after Lorraine "fell in love with it."
- She stated to us that she does not display her entire collection all at once.
- Client says that she only puts certain dolls out that correspond to the current "theme" for each specific time of year, or upcoming holiday.
- This doll was purchased in December of last year, and she thought that it would "be a great fit" for her "winter collection."

HOW LONG HAVE YOU BEEN AT THIS LOCATION?:
- Lorraine, and her (now deceased) husband purchased their home in the 1980s.
- She currently lives alone with her pet cat.

WHY DO YOU THINK THE OBJECT IS THE CAUSE OF THE PARANORMAL ACTIVITY:
- Lorraine states that she has lived alone in her home for the past 15 years.
- She claims that over the years, she will often feel her husband's presence visiting with her.

- Client also states that she is used to the feeling of him "coming around" because she always feels safe and at peace when it occurs.
- After purchasing the doll, she walked out of the store and immediately felt "an overwhelming feeling of anxiety."
- Lorraine stated that it was the same type of feeling that she gets when her husband is around, "but completely different at the same time."
- That experience was the start of a number of "bad omens."

UNEXPLAINED TEMPERATURE CHANGES:
- Lorraine noticed that whenever the "girl in the puffy coat" would appear, the room temperature would significantly drop with no explanation.
- Client states that this phenomena is something that she has never experienced before, until this entity started appearing.
- She also states that on the occasions when the temperature would drop, it would take an "abnormal" amount of time to heat the room back up again.

UNEXPLAINED ANOMALIES WITH ELECTRICAL DEVICES:
- On multiple occasions, Lorraine states that the lights would flicker "really fast for a second" whenever the "girl with the puffy coat would appear."
- On one occasion, two light bulbs burnt out after the experience.

UNEXPLAINED ILLNESS:
- None Reported.

MANIPULATION OF OBJECTS:
- Lorraine believes that the doll has moved twice on its own with no explanation.
- She states that her cat is not responsible. "He doesn't jump on the furniture because he is older."

UNEXPLAINED ODORS:
- None Reported.

UNEXPLAINED SOUNDS:

- Lorraine states that on a few occasions, she has heard "moving sounds" downstairs while she is in her bedroom at night.
- She states that she usually tries to tone it out by playing a CD.
- Again, she made it clear that it is not her cat because he sleeps in her room at night "in his cat house."

APPARITIONS/VISUAL ANOMALIES:

- Lorraine states that she has seen "a girl with black eyes and a puffy coat" on several occasions before something major happened in her life.
- The first time she saw this girl was right before she had suffered a serious car accident.
- She was driving down the road when "someone appeared in the middle of the road." She immediately swerved to avoid hitting them.
- She states that the person appeared so fast that she "didn't have time to process right away that she had no eyes, and looked like a black and white photo."
- When she swerved, she went off the road and hit a tree. Thankfully, she survived.
- On another occasion, the "girl with the puffy coat" appeared in the living room minutes before Lorraine had learned of her father's passing.
- She is extremely worried that this entity may have had something to do with it.
- The final experience was when Lorraine had seen this "bad omen" before she was about to go out with a friend. This caused her to cancel the outing, resulting in a "huge argument that permanently fractured the relationship."

UNEXPLAINED VOICES:

- Lorraine states that when the apparition appears, she never speaks to her.
- Her main belief is that the entity is just a "bad omen" that appears when something negative is about to happen.

- Client states that the only time she has heard a "paranormal voice" is when she had a "visitation" from her deceased husband.
- She explained to us that sometimes he will yell her name to "let her know that he is there with her."
- She states that she misses hearing him. She also believes that it is her fault that "he hasn't come around" since she brought the doll home.

PHYSICAL CONTACT:
- When Lorraine got into her car accident, she stated that "someone or something else" was in control of her car after she swerved, causing her to crash.
- She states that it was almost like she was "riding in a remote controlled car, being driven by someone else."
- Client states that at one point, she felt pressure on her arms while she was trying to correct the wheel (before the crash). She was pushing one way, while "an energy" was pushing the other way.

DESIRED RESULT / OUTCOME:
- Lorraine states that she wants the doll out of her life now.
- She states that she has major anxiety about seeing "the bad omen spirit" again.
- She also thinks that whatever "spirit or thing" is with the doll, is also blocking her husband from coming to visit her.
- Client believes that ever since she has brought the doll home, her husband's spirit has not shown up again.
- She is hoping that all will return to normal after the doll is "as far away as possible."

INVESTIGATOR NOTES:
- It seems like our client (Lorraine) is extremely affected after witnessing the apparition of "the girl with the puffy coat."
- We believe that removing the doll will help her mental state significantly.
- We have instructed her to email us if there are any other paranormal updates.

NOTES:

IMPORTANT UPDATE: Monday - February 15, 2021
EMAIL SENT TO PARANORMAL COUPLE ACCOUNT:
From: *************@email.com
Date: Monday - February 15, 2021 at 10:47:33 PM EST
To: contact@paranormalcouple.com
Subject: She Appeared!

Satori & Cody,
First off, I went to the post office today to send out the doll. According to them, you should be receiving it in a few days.
So about 30 minutes ago, I was just getting into bed when the lights flickered fast and the girl appeared.
I was so taken back, because I figured I would never see it again. This was the first time she spoke to me. She said "good riddance" and then disappeared.
I am hoping she means that...
Just wanted to update you. Thank you both again for all of your help, and for taking the doll off my hands. GOD BLESS.
-Lorraine

DATE OF ENTRY TO MUSEUM: Thursday - February 18, 2021
- Satori and I (Cody) have received the doll in the mail today.
- The doll was immediately placed into the quarantine room for observation.

CLIENT FOLLOW UP: Friday - March 5, 2021 - PHONE CALL
- I (Cody) was able to reach our client (Lorraine) over the phone.
- She states that the apparition has not appeared since the last occurrence (when the entity spoke.)
- She is very grateful, and extremely optimistic that she will get a visitation from her husband again soon.
- I (Cody) instructed her to contact us at any time if she is scared, or if she needs help and advice.

IMPORTANT UPDATE: Sunday - June 6, 2021

- It is important to note that this doll has been on display within our "Doll Section" of the museum for approximately two months now. There has been no abnormal activity, until now.
- Today, upon entering the museum, we were immediately met with a cold chill. This is something that often happens considering all of the items we have. Many pieces share claims of abnormal temperature fluctuations.
- This experience became more unusual when we noticed the doll.
- We found this doll in a completely different position than it had originally been placed in, since its first inclusion within the museum. It was almost completely facing the wall, in the opposite direction.
- We have no normal explanation as to how this may have occurred.

IMPORTANT UPDATE: Saturday - September 9, 2023

- Today was the first time that we had this doll on public display at an event in Massachusetts.
- When one individual was reading the description of "The Omen Doll," she immediately got cold chills. It was so significant that she notified us right away.
- Although we can't confirm that the occurrence was caused by this particular doll, it is ironic considering the story that accompanies it.

IMPORTANT UPDATE: Saturday - March 16, 2024

- This evening, Satori and I had a small investigation event located in Connecticut.
- During the event, an individual (who claimed to be a clairvoyant) approached us and claimed to have seen the spirit of a girl standing next to the doll.
- She also stated that an overwhelming "cold feeling" fell over her.
- We of course can't confirm these claims, but will take note of her experience in case someone else encounters something similar in the future.

THE BRIDGEWATER TRIANGLE ARTIFACT

For Jessica and her family, their small home in Freetown, Massachusetts, was meant to be a peaceful sanctuary. Surrounded by forest, this neighborhood seemed the perfect blend of suburban comfort, and spacious natural beauty. What was unknown to Jessica, however, was the fact that this home was situated at the edge of the infamous Bridgewater Triangle. This is a region notorious for its centuries long history of strange and terrifying occurrences.

For seven years, they enjoyed peaceful days and especially quiet nights. Nothing unusual would occur, accept for the occasional woodland sound, or a wandering animal in the yard.

That pattern of peace shattered in the summer of 2021. It started innocently enough. During an outing on the wooded trails of their property, Jessica's two children stumbled upon an unsettling discovery. Resting atop a moss-covered boulder was a handcrafted statue. At first glance, it seemed like a piece of folk art. The item appeared to be a carved log adorned with animal bones, a bird's wing, wax, and frayed rope. The object was weathered as if it had been there for years. It radiated mystery, and the children's curiosity got the better of them. They brought the statue home, completely unaware of the series of events they had just set into motion.

By that evening, their lives turned into a nightmare. During dinner, as the family routinely bowed their heads for prayer, the home was violently disrupted by the sound of galloping across the roof. The steps were loud and violently aggressive, seeming as if the ceiling was going to collapse. Panic set in for the family, but that was only the beginning.

Cold drafts began sweeping through the house, chilling everyone to the bone. Lights flickered erratically, and appliances began malfunctioning with no logical explanation. Worst of all were the voices, exact imitations of their own. The voices echoed throughout empty rooms, calling them by name. These eerie sounds felt malevolent, like a creature mimicking and playing mind games with its prey. These experiences left the family feeling both exposed and threatened.

Though they had placed the statue within the garage and left it untouched, its energy spread like a dark cloud over their home. The family's faith was a source of comfort, but it seemed to provoke whatever force had entered their space. Their prayers brought no relief; instead, they seemed to only invite more activity.

Soon, the disturbances started to escalate. The children suffered nightmares that left them screaming in their sleep. Jessica's car broke down unexpectedly, and the family's luck seemed to spiral downward in every possible way. As time passed, the darkness within their home took an emotional toll, leaving them exhausted, frightened, and desperate for help.

Jessica's breaking point came when her youngest child claimed to have seen something. It was described as a shadowy figure, lurking near the garage where the statue was stored. The shadow was tall, with glowing eyes that stared intensely before completely disappearing into the darkness. That was when Jessica reached out to the museum pleading for help. Her email was urgent, describing both her perspective on the current situation, and how her home no longer felt safe.

Questions began to mount. What was the purpose of this bizarre statue? Who had created it, and left it hidden in the woods? And, most chillingly, why was it so strongly attached to, and interested in the family living there?

The answers lay buried in the depths of the Bridgewater Triangle. Over the years, stories of strange lights, cryptid sightings, occult activity, and unexplained disappearances had turned the region into a hotspot of paranormal lore.

As we delved deeper into this case, each discovery unraveled another layer of the item's story. Local folklore hinted at rituals performed in the area, ceremonies meant to bind spirits or summon forces that should be left undisturbed. The artifact seemed to be associated with these tales, its construction being too deliberate to be a mere coincidence.

This is Case #071721, The Bridgewater Triangle Artifact.

CASE FILE

NAME: THE BRIDGEWATER TRIANGLE ARTIFACT

CASE#: 071721

DATE: July 17, 2021

CASE #: 071721 - The Bridgewater Triangle Artifact

CLIENT NAME: Jessica Hall
ALL OCCUPANTS AT LOCATION: Jessica (Client), Mike (Husband), 2 Children, 1 Dog, 1 Hamster, 2 Goldfish
DATE OF CASE: Summer of 2021
DATE CLIENT OBTAINED OBJECT: July of 2021
CLIENT LOCATION: Freetown, Massachusetts
LOCATION OBTAINED: Woods located behind their home
OBJECT MANUFACTURE ORIGIN: Handmade

POINT OF CONTACT
EMAIL SENT TO PARANORMAL COUPLE ACCOUNT:
From: ***********@email.com
Date: July 17, 2021 at 4:16:30 PM EST
To: contact@paranormalcouple.com (WEBSITE)
Subject: Please Help us if you can!

Hello, we recently got your name from a neighbor who said he met you at one of your library presentations last Autumn. He told us that you were the right people to call, so I hope you can help us.
We live in Freetown, MA, and are dealing with some Satanic trespassers on our property.
Our property line borders a large forest that unfortunately has a bad reputation for satanic worshipping and other cult activities. It has now come way too close for comfort. We need something removed from our home IMMEDIATELY. Please contact me at your earliest convenience! THANK YOU.

Jessica Hall

PRELIMINARY PHONE INTERVIEW

PHONE INTERVIEW BY: Cody Ray DesBiens & Satori Hawes
DATE: Friday - July 23, 2021
CLIENT NAME: Jessica Hall
PHONE NUMBER: ***-***-****
EMAIL: ***********@email.com

DESCRIPTION OF OBJECT IN QUESTION:

- Handmade - presumed occult / ceremonial item.
- Primary material is a log standing upright with symbols carved into it.
- Other observed materials include a bird wing, animal jaw bones, wax, herbs, and rope.

HOW WAS THE OBJECT OBTAINED:

- About a week ago, the client (Jessica's) husband (Mike), and their two kids, were riding 4 wheelers on the wood trails behind their home.
- It is important to note that these trails are on Jessica and Mike's property.
- At some point, the kids came across a large rock with an "occult item" sitting on top of it.
- They had no knowledge of what it was, and thought it looked "cool." The kids brought it into the garage unbeknownst to Jessica and Mike.

WHY DO YOU THINK THE OBJECT IS THE CAUSE OF THE PARANORMAL ACTIVITY:

- A few hours after the object was brought into the garage by the kids, the family took a seat around their dining room table for dinner.
- Being a Christian family, they all bowed their heads and began to say a routine prayer before they ate.
- As soon as Mike began the prayer, Jessica states that "it sounded like a heavy horse was running on the roof, and going to crash through."
- This of course frightened the entire family.
- Immediately, Jessica and Mike ran outside to see if they could find an explanation.

- As they opened the garage door to exit the house, sitting on top of a crate was the item.
- Jessica states that as soon as they saw it, they "felt their hearts drop," and slammed the door shut.
- Client states that they instantly knew that "whatever that thing is, was the cause of what had just happened."
- This was the first instance of paranormal activity ever occurring in the home.
- Other paranormal events soon followed.
- The family agreed to not go in the garage until it has been removed.

HOW LONG HAVE YOU BEEN AT THIS LOCATION?:
- Jessica and her family have lived in their home for the past 7 years.
- They explained that they love their home and neighborhood very much, but this situation has "put a dark and dangerous cloud of evil" over them.
- They have never experienced anything paranormal before.

UNEXPLAINED TEMPERATURE CHANGES:
- Jessica states that she recalls getting "cold chills" when they opened the door to the garage.
- She also expressed that they have central air conditioning, but "this was a different kind of cold."

UNEXPLAINED ANOMALIES WITH ELECTRICAL DEVICES:
- The chandelier in the main entryway has been flickering on and off for the past 2 days with no explanation.
- The garage where the item is being stored has two automatic, remote garage doors.
- Jessica states that on multiple occasions (especially when it is dark out) both garage doors have started sporadically opening and closing by themselves.
- This is something that has never happened before.

UNEXPLAINED ILLNESS:
- None Reported.

MANIPULATION OF OBJECTS:
- On one occasion, the chandelier in the home's entryway began swinging in a circle with no explanation.

UNEXPLAINED ODORS:
- Jessica reports that she has experienced an overwhelming smell of "dirt."

UNEXPLAINED SOUNDS:
- Besides the sound of something galloping on the roof, there has been a plethora of other unexplained sounds.
- On multiple occasions, the family has heard what sounds like doors slamming shut, even though all of them remain open.
- The sound of knocking on the second floor bedroom windows has been heard on 3 occasions.
- When the knocking happens, it occurs on multiple windows at the same time for approximately 5 seconds.
- Scratching noises throughout the home have also been reported.
- The family claims that a multitude of these sounds (combined) will occur on occasion when they pray as a family.
- The client and family claim that the noises sound as if they are "surrounding the house."

UNEXPLAINED VOICES:
- On at least 5 different occasions, each child has come downstairs claiming that their name was called from the first floor.
- They claim that the voice imitates both the client, and her husband.
- This has begun to unsettle the entire family.
- The kids are afraid that they will come downstairs and be greeted with "something else," rather than their parents.

APPARITIONS/VISUAL ANOMALIES:
- None Reported.

PHYSICAL CONTACT:
- None Reported.

OTHER NOTES:

- The children have been having nightmares ever since they brought the item into the garage.
- Sometimes they will wake up screaming.
- Jessica also feels like her family is dealing with a string of "bad luck."
- Since the item has been in the garage, they all try to leave during the day (as a family) to "escape the evil."
- They have begun to notice that car trouble has become a regular occurance. Some examples are - flat tires, windshield wipers flying off of the car, and many close calls with animals running into the road.

DESIRED RESULT / OUTCOME:

- Jessica and her family want the object GONE as soon as possible. Client states that they want "the house to turn back into a home again."

INVESTIGATOR NOTES:

- Due to the fact that the family is so terrified, we have decided to schedule an in person visit to remove the item as soon as possible.
- We have also recommended that the entire family continue to use their faith to help calm the situation. We believe that intention is a powerful tool.
- We also instructed the family to speak out loud, and set ground rules if the activity gets intense, or when they feel overwhelmed.

IN-PERSON VISIT TO LOCATION

DATE OF VISIT: Sunday - July 25, 2021
INVESTIGATORS PRESENT: Cody Ray DesBiens & Satori Hawes
LOCATION RESIDENTS PRESENT: Jessica (client), Mike (husband), 2 Dogs, 2 Fish (kids were at a neighbors house)

PRELIMINARY NOTES UPON ARRIVAL:

- Satori and I were met by the client (Jessica) and her husband (Mike) at the front door of their home.
- They were beyond thankful we were there, but you could tell that they seemed drained.
- They invited us inside for a tour of their home, but asked that we "don't talk about the thing" while inside of the house.
- Once the tour was finished, we went out into the front yard to talk about the object in question.
- They claimed that it felt extremely difficult to get up, and get the family ready for church that morning.
- Jessica states that it felt like all energy had been drained out of the family, and that they were "walking with weights on their feet."
- They pushed through it, and claimed to have felt "much better" when they arrived at their church.
- Mike then gave us permission to enter their garage, and remove the artifact.
- Once removed, and placed into our vehicle, you could notice a change (for the better) with Jessica's emotional state.

CLOSING NOTES OF IN-PERSON VISIT:

- While we were driving home, the family called to express how much better the home felt now that the object was removed.
- We plan to check in with the family after the object is out of quarantine. This will be in approximately two weeks.

NOTES:

DATE OF ENTRY TO MUSEUM: Sunday - July 25, 2021

- Today, Satori and I placed the item within the quarantine room to observe it for the next two weeks
- Satori has also completed some research as to what some of the symbols carved into the wood could be interpreted as.
- It is difficult to say what the overall meaning behind the artifact was, because we weren't there to witness the ritual.

POSSIBLE SYMBOL
MEANINGS

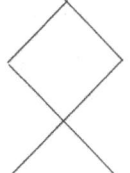

Possession, Heritage, Justice, Honor

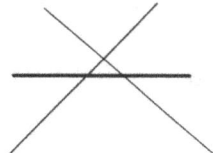

Confusion

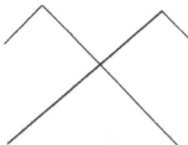

Jumis: Strength, Wealth, Success,
Safety, Prosperity

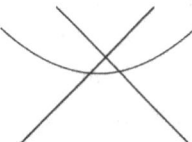

War & Conflict

✳ The symbol of "Jumis" on the object is an upside down version
of this symbol, which could possibly give the opposite meaning.

✳ These symbols are known as pagan runes, "Jumis" being more
specifically Baltic. This statue could be linked to possible Baltic
Witchcraft.

✳ This item could have been placed upon the rock to set
intentions upon the land (in which the house sits), or the
house itself, as it was facing that exact direction. We cannot
say for certain at this time.

CLIENT FOLLOW UP: Saturday - August 14, 2021 - PHONE CALL
- Today, Satori & myself were able to reach our client (Jessica) over the telephone.
- She stated that everything has completely gone back to normal.
- They wish to move on from the experience, and ask for full confidentiality. They worry that their contact with us, and handling of the situation, may gain judgment from their community. They are extremely grateful that the item is gone.

IMPORTANT UPDATE: September & October of 2021
- Over the past few months, we have displayed the artifact at a few of our traveling events.
- On multiple occasions, at different events, many people claim to feel an energy "emerging" from the item.
- Some individuals have felt peace with the energy, but most felt anxious and drained.
- Some individuals have also claimed to feel as though they need to "hold" the item. We do not allow any handling of this object.

IMPORTANT UPDATE: July of 2022
- This month, we had the artifact on display at two separate events.
- At both events, this item became the popular topic of discussion because of the way different individuals felt near the statue.
- Some people felt as if they needed to stand closer to the artifact, almost as if it was pulling them in. One individual claimed to have gotten "extremely hot" when walking by this item.

IMPORTANT UPDATE: Sunday - November 5, 2023
- This weekend, the Bridgewater Triangle artifact was on display at an event in New Jersey.
- One individual (who entered our exhibit room) felt a dramatic pull towards the statue. This feeling was so significant, that she asked multiple times to hold the object.
- Satori and I thought that it was best for her to step away from the table, hoping to detach her from the item, and any possible energy.
- After standing in the hall for a few minutes, she acknowledged that something definitely felt "a little off."

SPIRITUAL PROTECTION TOOLS

Spiritual protection tools vary by belief system, but share a goal of shielding against negativity. Here are some common examples:

Holy Water:
Used in Christianity to bless oneself, and ward off evil.

Crystals:
Black tourmaline, obsidian, and amethyst absorb and repel negative energy.

Salt:
Used in many cultures (Himalayan, sea, or blessed salt) to create protective spiritual barriers.

Talisman or Amulets:
Examples include a cross, evil eye, protection bottle, or Hamsa hand for spiritual defense.

holy water

THE PARANORMAL COUPLE'S

HAUNTED
MUSEUM
OF

OBJECTS, ODDITIES AND CURIOSITIES

THE MONKEY PAW

Throughout history, humans have consistently shown an undeniable interest in the unknown. The promise of power, the ability to shape reality to your will, and the hope of finding a solution to a seemingly impossible problem is tempting. This temptation, however, has led countless people to venture into dangerous territory. Emily Nelson's story is a cautionary tale for anyone who's ever thought about dabbling in rituals, or objects of power. Without an extensive understanding of the subject, the unknown can lead to dark places far beyond our imagination.

Normally, when someone donates an item to our collection, we follow a strict process: interviews, site visits if possible, and a detailed investigation into the history of the object. But Emily wasn't looking for that. She wasn't concerned about study, context, or answers. She knew what she had been dealing with, and she just wanted the item gone. Emily felt that it was best if the object was both out of her life, and out of reach. Her urgency was abundantly clear, and the museum was more than willing to help.

Emily's letter arrived, tucked into a package that contained a small decorative box. Inside of the box sat what is claimed to be a shriveled monkey's paw, an object of infamous legend. From the moment that we opened the box, the air seemed substantially heavier. Emily's desperation radiated off of every line of her letter, a confession from someone who had been pushed far beyond her limits.

Emily's story wasn't unusual in its beginnings. She was a person at her breaking point, facing financial struggles, and consumed by hopelessness. The internet, with its endless promises of solutions, led her to a dark corner. The ominous monkey's paw was presented as a path that could fix all of Emily's problems. The ritual seemed simple enough, just a few steps to activate the paw's supposed powers, and grant the user a set of wishes. Emily admitted that she had no real knowledge of rituals and the forces she was attempting to manipulate, but desperation has a funny way of silencing any hesitation.

The results seemed swift, and at first, it was almost miraculous. Emily's wish for money came true in the form of a big $10,000 scratch ticket win. But the success was short lived, shadowed by a series of events that quickly showed Emily how wishes can, sometimes, carry a terrible price. These experiences drove home the realization that she had tampered with forces beyond her understanding.

Emily's story is a reminder of the dangers surrounding engagement with the unknown. Rituals, ceremonies, artifacts, and occult practices are not simple tools, they are conduits for energy and intention that can easily spiral far beyond control. Whether you believe in curses, residual energy, or the psychological toll of both guilt and fear, the results and consequences seem to be undeniable. Emily's experience didn't just affect her, but actually rippled out, affecting people that she loved most.

When we accepted the monkey's paw into our museum collection, we knew that it wasn't just another artifact to display. It was a strong warning in physical form. Emily's letter now accompanies the paw within our "Dark Room." It serves as a powerful example of the dangers surrounding meddling with forces we don't understand.

If there's one takeaway from Emily's story, it's this: curiosity and distress can lead to dangerous things. The promise of power and a quick solution often comes at a cost we're not fully prepared to pay. As Emily put it, *"Spread the word that people should not dabble in ritual things if they have no idea what they are getting themselves into... like me."*

This is case #102622, The Monkey Paw. This object may be out of Emily's life for good, but the lesson it holds remains as relevant as ever. For those tempted by the strange and mysterious, let Emily's story serve as a chilling warning to you: some doors are best left unopened.

CASE FILE

NAME: THE MONKEY'S PAW

CASE#: 102622

DATE: October 10, 2022

Thank you so much for taking this away for me.

My life has been financially miserable for the past 10 years or so. Ever since my breakup with my ex-fiance, things seemed to really go downhill. I am in so much debt that I seriously feel trapped in a 100 foot hole. The hole has now gotten much deeper.

It's amazing how outrageous someone can act in times of disparity...

I sourced out this monkey paw because I read online of a ritual involving one. The person who wrote the article claimed that this was the only thing that worked for him. It was extremely hard to find an authentic one, but I eventually did. I read online that after doing a small ritual, I would be able to make as many wishes as the number of claws on the paw. After receiving the paw, I spent days preparing for the first ritual. I wanted to make sure everything was correct so I wouldn't mess it up. Finally I was ready, and I put my first wish out into the universe. I waited, and waited and nothing seemed to happen right away, until it all hit me like a train.

The first wish was for money. I needed to start paying off all of this debt, so I wished for a lot of it. I went out and bought a scratch ticket a few days later and won 10 grand. I couldn't believe that it had actually worked. An unexplainably weird feeling fell over me and on my way to the state lottery to cash the ticket, I got in a horrible car accident. My car hydroplaned over the embankment and it flipped 3 or 4 times. I broke my nose from the airbag and cracked a couple of my ribs. The car was totaled, but that scratch off was the only thing on my mind. When i got back home from the hospital, I unzipped my purse to find that the ticket was now missing. It was no longer in my purse where I had put it. I dumped the contents onto the table and shuffled through the stuff over and over again throwing things around my kitchen in rage. I had no idea how it had escaped a zipped up pocket book. It was gone. I was so upset and frantic on where that small piece of cardboard worth so much money had gone. I had to have that money back. In a panic, I did my second ritual rite then and there and made my wish to find that scratch ticket, or receive more money. Again, nothing happened at first, but a few days later, it hit me like a train again.

I was in my bedroom and grabbed one of my pillows to change the pillowcase. When I looked down I couldn't believe my eyes. The scratch ticket was sitting there on the bed. The same bed that I sleep in everyday. It just appeared like magic. There is no possible way to even begin to find a normal explanation as to how this happened. That weird feeling fell over me again, but I was more concerned about getting my money. Having no car, I called my parents to ask for a ride. My mom answered the phone and I started to explain to her how I needed a ride as soon as possible to get my money. Well as soon as I said the word "money," she started to scream and yell "Oh My God!" The phone hung up and I was now in a panic. I kept calling back over and over again and finally my mom answered, crying and screaming. To keep a long story short, as soon as I said "money," my dad dropped to the floor and had a massive heart attack right in front of my mom. She had to hang up on me to call an ambulance.

When I found out what had happened, that weird feeling hit me again, worse than before. Something inside of me told me that the monkey paw was to blame for everything bad that was happening in my life. This now made me extremely nervous to cash in the scratch ticket. To my surprise, I ripped it up and decided that I needed to get rid of the paw so I wouldn't have the temptation to make another wish. In my opinion, the money was much less important than my dad's life and I wasn't taking any more chances. He barely survived the heart attack, and I can't imagine what could happen next if I made a third wish. I am done.

Thank you for releasing me from this curse that I got myself into. If I contact you in the future to have it back, PLEASE DO NOT EVER SEND IT BACK TO ME NO MATTER WHAT I SAY. KEEP THIS LETTER AS PROOF THAT I DO NOT EVER WANT IT BACK. Put it under glass and don't let anyone touch the thing! Please spread the word that people should not dabble in ritual things if they have no idea what they are getting themselves into...like me.

Emily Nelson

The concept of wishing on a monkey's paw traces its origins to "The Monkey's Paw," a fictional short story by W.W. Jacobs. it was first published in 1902.

There are multiple similar cases found across the world regarding individuals making wishes with a monkey paw.

W.W. Jacobs

Other Similarities in Folklore and Mythology

* **Greek Mythology:** The tale of King Midas, who wished that everything he touched would turn to gold, only to realize that his wish was a curse.

* **Arabic Folklore:** The concept of djinn (genies) granting wishes. This often involves similar cautionary twists, where wishes are granted literally, or with unforeseen consequences.

* **European Folktales:** Stories of magical objects such as cursed rings or talismans, often involving unintended consequences for those who use them.

REFLECTIONS
OF THE UNSEEN

As we walked through the museum one final time before locking the door for the night, the air seemed heavier than usual. It was as though the artifacts themselves were listening, aware that their stories were being told. Each object rested quietly in its specific space, yet their presence was detectable. These aren't mere items, they are memories etched in wood, glass, fabric, and bone. They are reminders of lives once lived, moments now lost, and unseen forces that influence us all.

Reflecting on the journey that we shared in assembling this book, we couldn't help but admire the diversity of the stories that these items carried. Some brought terror, others mystery, and a few had brought strong, even beautiful connections to loved ones who had passed on.

The objects we've chronicled here, from the glass eye, to the whistle crafted by witches, displays not only a brush with the supernatural, but also a fragment of the human condition. These stories weren't just about fear and the unknown, they were also about resilience, love, grief, and the search for answers. But for every case that we've shared with you in these pages, there are countless more waiting to be discovered. The emails continue to come, the packages still arrive, and each box continues to contain something both extraordinary, and unexplainable. People reach out to the museum, not just with objects, but with their fears, confusion, and their hopes that someone can listen and make sense of it all.

We've learned that haunted objects are more than physical things, possibly imprinted with strange energy, they are bridges. These bridges connect the past and present, the living and dead, what we understand, and what we cannot quite grasp. They show us that the unknown is not something to be feared, but rather, something to be explored.

The museum has grown significantly over the years, and so has our understanding of what it means to interact with these pieces. Some we have been able to study and openly share, others remain wrapped in mystery, and hidden away from the public due to their dark nature. We have come to accept that not everything will have a definitive answer, or a willingness to tell its story. That doesn't stop us from trying, however.

Perhaps you have your own story to share. Perhaps an object in your possession holds a special past that you've yet to uncover. If so, know that you are not alone in your curiosity. We remain here, guarding these stories, ready to listen and learn when we are needed.

So the museum is quiet now. The lights are dimmed, and the air is still. The energy within these walls, however, never fades. The objects may rest, but their tales continue to echo throughout the space. The spirits await another chance to interact with new souls, watching their stories send chills down more unsuspecting spines. It's only a matter of time.

So this brings us to the end of this book, but it is *not* the end of our journey. The unknown calls to us, and as usual, we cannot help but answer.

Until next time,

"Not all stories end when the last page is turned.
Some linger... waiting to be told again."

www.ingramcontent.com/pod-product-compliance
Lightning Source LLC
Chambersburg PA
CBHW071708120626
46550CB00001B/145